Kansas

KANSAS BY ROAD

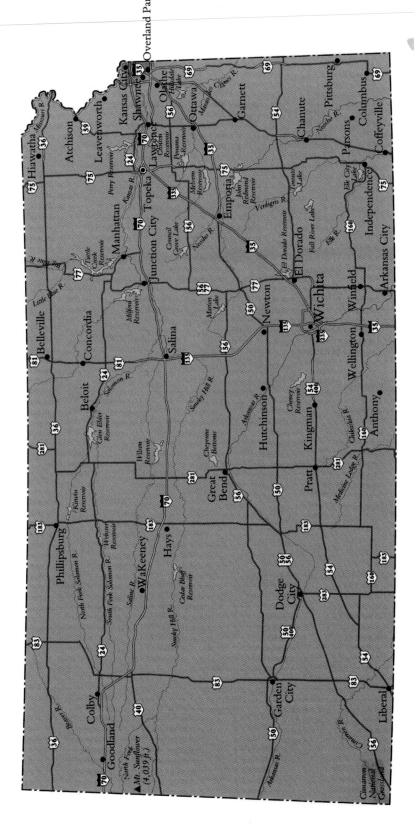

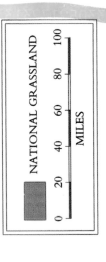

NATIONAL GRASSLAND

MILES

0   20   40   60   80   100

N
W   E
S

Celebrate the States

Kansas

Ruth Bjorklund and Trudi Strain Trueit

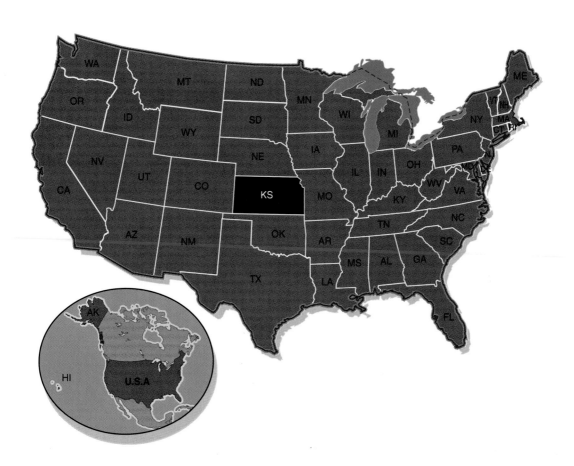

Marshall Cavendish
Benchmark

New York

Marshall Cavendish Benchmark
99 White Plains Road
Tarrytown, NY 10591-5502
www.marshallcavendish.us

All Internet addresses were correct and accurate at the time of printing.

Library of Congress Cataloging-in-Publication Data
Bjorklund, Ruth.
Kansas / by Ruth Bjorklund and Trudi Strain Trueit. — 2nd ed.
p. cm. — (Celebrate the states)
Summary: "Provides comprehensive information on the geography, history, wildlife,
governmental structure, economy, cultural diversity, peoples, religion, and
landmarks of Kansas"—Provided by publisher.
Includes bibliographical references and index.
ISBN 978-0-7614-3400-9
1. Kansas—Juvenile literature. I. Trueit, Trudi Strain. II. Title.

F681.3.B56 2009
978.1—dc22
2008005537

Editor: Christine Florie
Publisher: Michelle Bisson
Art Director: Anahid Hamparian
Series Designer: Adam Mietlowski

Photo research by Connie Gardner

Cover photo by Mark Newman/Alamy

The photographs in this book are used by permission and through the courtesy of: *Corbis:* Medio Images, back cover; Phil Schermeister, 11, 79; David Muench, 12; Eric Nguyen, 16, 23; Michele Westmorland, 18; Bettmann, 30, 41, 45, 119, 121, 125, 129; R.S. Kellogg, 34; Corbis, 37, 44, 120; Philip Gould, 48, 105 (T); Richard Cummins, 64; Dave G. Houser, 87; Lisa O'Connor, 117; Tim Rue, 127; *AP Photo:* The Hutchinson News, Travis Morisse, 50, 70, 89; The Topeka Capital-Journal, Mike Shepherd, 55; Charles Riedel, 57, 95; The Independence Daily Reporter, 58; Hays Daily News, Kim Rowland, 61; Kiichiro Sato, 73; The Salina Journal, Ryan Soderlin, 76; Jeff Cooper, 78; Carlos Osorio, 88; Orlin Wagner, 92, 102; Cliff Schiappa, 94. *Joel Satore Photography,* 52; *Danita Delimont:* Mark Gibson, 66; David R. Frazier, 81; *Art Life Images:* Harland J. Schuster, 103, 116; *Getty Images:* Altrendo Nature, 8; Hulton Archive, 28; Richard W. Kelley, 123; *Tom Bean:* 13, 133; *Minden Pictures:* Tim Fitzharris, 15; Jim Brandenburg, 105 (B); Sumio Harada, 109; Konrad Wothe, 113; *Art Resource:* Smithsonian American Art Museum, 26; *The Granger Collection:* 33. 42. 74; *SuperStock:* agefotostock, 17; *John Elk Photography:* 97; *The Image Works:* Jenny Hager, 21; Andre Jenny, 96, 135, 137; Topham, 131; *Alamy:* North Wind Picture Archives, 24, 29, 39; Michael Snell, 90, 99.

Printed in Malaysia
1 3 5 6 4 2

Contents

Kansas Is . . .

Kansas is wide-open spaces . . .

"I was born on the prairie, where the wind blew free and there was nothing to break the light of the sun. I was born where there were no enclosures and where everything drew a free breath."
 —Parra-Wa-Samen (Ten Bears), Comanche Indian, treaty speech, 1872

. . . and boundless skies.

"Life and prosperity depend upon that sky, which can destroy a season's crops in a few hours, by hail or blizzards or tornadoes or a relentlessly burning sun that can desiccate the land like an Old Testament curse."
 —William Inge, playwright

It is where independence meets innovation.

"When anything is going to happen in this country, it happens first in Kansas. Abolitionism, prohibition, Populism . . . these things came popping out of Kansas like bats out of hell."
 —William Allen White, Kansas newspaper publisher, 1922

And where dreamers meet their destinies.

"The country here is just beautiful here, and by the way, we have the best claim around here . . . I think I will like Kansas."
 —Flora Moorman Heston, homesteader, 1885

Kansas touches the senses . . .

"The ever-changing prairie is covered with the colors of wildflowers; the sunflower, of course, and the buttercup, primrose, wild daisy, gayfeather, and wild onion—each a different color and each lasting only a few days."

> —Patti DeLano, travel writer; *Off the Beaten Path: Kansas*

. . . as well as the soul.

"I'm so very proud to be a Kansan. It's difficult to put into words, because—as you know—the pride of being a Kansan is really something you feel."

> —Kathleen Sebelius, Governor, 2003

"It is only necessary for us to be well informed of the history of our state to make us love her, to make us devoted to her, to make us patriotic."

> —William E. Connelley, Kansas historian

In Kansas people speak proudly of the infinite skies, of the far-reaching prairies, and of a history so alive, it seems to be breathing. Despite the challenging conditions—parching sun, floods, droughts, blizzards, thunderstorms, and tornadoes—Kansans take pride in their state. "Even though Kansas's environment is sometimes rough," says Megan Tunget, thirteen, of Lawrence, "it is just preparing me for what may come in the future." Emporia teacher Denise Low calls Kansas a place "beyond all time where only the best part of the human spirit walks, touching both earth and sky at once." Kansas is, simply put, the heartbeat of the nation.

Chapter One

A Journey Through Kansas

Kansas may, at first glance, seem like endless prairies and wheat fields. After all, no other state in the nation grows more wheat than Kansas. But take a closer look at the Sunflower State, and you will see much more than rolling waves of croplands and grasses. From labyrinthine valleys to red buttes, from swift rivers to stunning rock towers, Kansas is a land of beautiful contrasts.

At 82,282 square miles, Kansas is the fifteenth-largest state in the United States. It is shaped like a rectangle, except where the winding Missouri River cuts into its northeastern corner. The state is 411 miles wide and 208 miles long. Kansas is bordered by Colorado to the west, Nebraska to the north, Missouri to the east, and Oklahoma to the south.

Kansas is not flat. It gradually increases in elevation, from 679 feet above sea level in the Verdigris River Valley in the east to 4,039 feet at Mount Sunflower in the west, the highest point in the state.

Cornstalks frame a field of ripe wheat in Kansas, which is one of the major wheat producers in North America.

HEART OF THE U.S.A.

Want to stand smack in the middle of the lower forty-eight states? Trek to north-central Kansas, where a stone monument outside the tiny town of Lebanon marks the geographic center of the contiguous states (when Alaska and Hawaii joined the Union in 1959, the center of all fifty states shifted to a spot in rural South Dakota). The nation's geodetic center, which takes into account the curve of Earth's surface, is found at Meades Ranch, about 40 miles south of Lebanon. Since the early twentieth century, government surveyors have used the Meades Ranch Triangulation Station in Osborne County to map the continental United States.

Kansas is made up mainly of two geographical areas: the Great Plains and the Central Lowland. The Great Plains cover the central and western two-thirds of the state, while the Central Lowland makes up much of the eastern third of Kansas.

EASTERN KANSAS

Gentle hills, woodlands, shallow valleys, and prairies can be found in eastern Kansas. More than ten thousand years ago, North America's last ice age ended. The melting glaciers and shifting rock formed the rolling hills and bluffs that characterize the northeastern corner of the state.

Two major rivers flow west to east, the Kansas (also called the Kaw) in the north and the Arkansas in the south. The Missouri River winds along the state's northeast corner. Along its banks are marshes and thick, humid forests of elm, hickory, and cottonwood that shelter ducks, beaver, and woodland birds. The Missouri was a major thoroughfare for early traders and settlers, and depots and towns sprang up along it. Today, the state's third-largest city, Kansas City, sits along the river. Eastern Kansas is also home to the thriving cities of Olathe, Overland Park, Lawrence, and Topeka, the capital of the Sunflower State.

Grasslands once extended from Canada to Texas and from Ohio to the Rocky Mountains. Farmers and ranchers turned so much of the grassland into cropland that little remains untouched. Too rocky to plow, eastern Kansas's Flint Hills contain the largest expanse of wild tallgrass left in the nation. In the Flint Hills, bluestem grasses, wildflowers, and limestone- and flint-specked mesas are a refuge for a colorful array of prairie birds, such as the upland sandpiper, eastern meadowlark, and greater prairie chicken. The prairie's forty species of grasses are home to many species of animals, including badgers, foxes, bobcats, deer, and wild turkey.

The Flint Hills are not suitable for farming and therefore have remained a vast region of rolling hills, flowers, and grasses.

SAVING THE TALLGRASS PRAIRIE

Of the 400,000 square miles of tallgrass prairies that once stretched across North America, fewer than 16,000 square miles remain—much of it in Kansas's Flint Hills. In 1996 the Tallgrass Prairie National Preserve was established to protect this valuable ecosystem. At the 11,000-acre park you can see more than four hundred different kinds of plants and wildflowers, go bird-watching (there are 150 species), or stroll through a rocky prairie. Be careful not to lose your way. Big bluestem grass can grow to a height of 10 feet!

South and east of the Flint Hills are colorful limestone and shale ridges called the Osage Cuestas. *Cuesta* is the Spanish word for "hillside." On one side the Osage Cuestas are steep and craggy, while on the other tractors plow gentle, rolling fields.

Kansas's southeast corner is nothing like the vast golden prairie. Densely forested, wet, and hilly, it is part of the Ozark Mountains, which extend south and east.

CENTRAL KANSAS

Venturing into central Kansas, you are reminded of the ancient inland seas that covered the region 80 million years ago. Though the water has disappeared, sandy beaches (and fossils) have endured. High winds have blown the sand into colossal dunes. "It's so sandy that when the pioneers first tried to irrigate their crops by building canals in their fields, the water in the canals drained out right through the sand!" laughs historian Barbara Brackman.

This is Arkansas River country (pronounced "Ar-KAN-sas" in this state). The Arkansas River begins high in the Colorado Rockies and sweeps grandly through southern Kansas in a giant arc. The center of the arc is called the Great Bend. Two incredible wetlands, Cheyenne Bottoms and Quivira National Wildlife Refuge, are located nearby.

The Cheyenne Bottoms wetlands is a habitat that attracts diverse wildlife.

Although they may seem desolate to humans, these rich marshes play host to a teeming horde of waterfowl. In spring and fall, half of all of North America's shorebirds stop to feed on tasty Kansas bloodworms. This feast attracts many of the nation's endangered and threatened birds, including peregrine falcons, bald eagles, whooping cranes, and piping plovers.

North and west, beyond the Great Bend marshes, the land returns to rolling prairies and hills. The Smoky Hill River curves and meanders across the central plains. Sometimes, the river's course shifts and a section of river gets blocked off, forming a small, curved lake. Most of Kansas's natural lakes are these so-called oxbow lakes.

Wichita, the state's largest city, is located where the Arkansas and Little Arkansas rivers meet, in south-central Kansas. Established as a trading post in 1867, Wichita became part of the Chisholm Trail. The trail was a major cattle-driving route from Texas to Abilene, Kansas. In its cow town heyday as many as 100,000 longhorn cattle passed through the city during the trail-driving season.

Throughout central Kansas are limestone deposits. One of the largest is in the Chalk Hills. Limestone is soft when it is underground, but once exposed to the air, it hardens. Because trees are rare in this part of Kansas, the resourceful pioneers used limestone as a building material. They carved limestone blocks for use in fences, bridges, and barns, many of which are still in use today.

WESTERN KANSAS

While eastern Kansas is known for sweeping meadows of long and lush grasses, called the prairies, western Kansas is defined by its short and flat grasses—the plains. The dividing point between the prairies and the plains lies at 100 degrees longitude, an invisible north-south line near Dodge City

FLOWER POWER

Take a drive down a country road in Kansas in the summer and you will understand why its nickname is the Sunflower State. *Helianthus*, or wild native sunflowers, are everywhere. The Kansas variety of sunflower is a bushy plant featuring hundreds of small, gold blooms. Hot, dry summers and fertile soil also makes Kansas the perfect place for growing traditional sunflowers (those with a big, single bloom on each tall stalk). Kansas farmers cultivate sunflowers for use in human snack foods, margarine, cooking oil, birdseed, and fuel. Kansas produces more than 450 billion pounds of sunflowers every year!

in the west. The prairies are best for growing crops, while the plains are excellent for raising livestock.

Buffalo grass and tumbleweed sage are common in the High Plains of western Kansas. There is little rain or surface water here. It is one of the least populated places in the entire country. "It's so empty out here, if you see another person, you have to acknowledge it," explains a Scott County resident. "We do the two-fingered wave; that's your two forefingers lifted off the steering wheel."

Winds hurl across the plains, and without trees or other barriers, they pick up extraordinary speed. It is no wonder Kansas chose to locate a 12,000-acre wind farm here. In 2001 the first windmill at the Gray County Wind Farm, near Montezuma, began turning. The average wind speed at the farm is about 20 miles per hour. One hundred seventy turbines generate enough electricity to power 33,000 homes.

In the southwestern corner of the state is the Cimarron National Grassland. The 108,000-acre park is the largest area of public land in the state. The grassland was once prime farmland, until severe drought and the dust storms of

These windmills rotate with great speed as a storm approaches.

the 1930s devastated the region. Here, visitors can climb to the top of Point of Rocks, the third-highest point in Kansas, to gaze out across the plains and scan for elk and antelope.

In the western Kansas Badlands, impressive limestone rocks tower over the surrounding plains. Monument Rocks, sometimes called the Chalk Pyramids, are a favorite tourist destination. Sculpted into eerie archways and monoliths by wind and water millions of years ago, many of the limestone formations rise 70 feet above the dusty valley floor.

The Monument Rocks were once part of an ancient seafloor.

WHERE ARE THE EARPLUGS?

Kansas wheat fields, grasslands, and gardens are home to hundreds of species of insects, including the noisy cicada (si-KAY-duh). Cicadas are large winged insects related to aphids and leafhoppers. They live most of their lives burrowed in the ground and only leave their hideaways to mate. Some come out after seven years, some after thirteen, and some after seventeen. Aboveground, cicadas live in trees. Most years their arrival is only briefly noticed. But when two or more cycles coincide, watch out! Each group of cicadas has its own special chirp, and when there are two or more groups, their chirping becomes a pounding, daylong din. Insect expert George Byers calls it cicada psychosis. Once the cicadas mate, the adults die. When two or more groups mate in the same year, there are a lot of dead bodies. In 1998 the thirteen-year and the seventeen-year cycles came together. "The carcasses were so plentiful, you could scoop them off the ground with a bucket! Dogs love to eat them,"

laughs Lawrence gardener Marilyn Teeter. "My neighbor's dog ate so many he got sick and had to wear a muzzle!" Cicadas do not typically destroy crops or gardens, but they can certainly be annoying.

WATER WOES

"In eastern Kansas, people debate water-quality issues. In western Kansas, people fight over who gets to use how much," says Charles Jones, who was once the state's director of environment. "In eastern Kansas, we're better off than we were ten years ago, and ten years from now, we should be better off still." But in western Kansas it seems the problems are just beginning.

More than ten thousand years ago, many rivers ran down from the Rocky Mountains and over the High Plains. The sand and gravel beds that make up the High Plains acted like a giant sponge, soaking up the river water and storing it underground. Today this underground water, called the Ogallala Aquifer, lies beneath a region extending from South Dakota to Texas. It is capable of holding a quadrillion gallons of water. This region averages only 18 inches of rain a year, so the Ogallala Aquifer is the main water source for the High Plains region. Since pioneer days, people have been taking water out of the aquifer. "We say they are mining water," says Jones. "It's fossil water, historical water. If we drained it all, it would take six thousand years to replace."

In this region, wheat grows in seemingly endless rows. But some farming methods waste this precious water. Jones explains, "When you fly over the west you see those big green circles on the ground. That's center-pivot irrigation. With it, farmers can irrigate fields that aren't flat enough for irrigation pipes. Trouble is, those center pivots spray water all over the place. Most of it evaporates before it ever hits the ground." Farmers are currently using the water twenty-five times faster than it can be replaced. Many rivers, springs, and wetlands fed by the aquifer have gone dry. In some places, even the Arkansas River has been reduced to a trickle. "We're really trying to come up with solutions," contends Jones.

LAND AND WATER

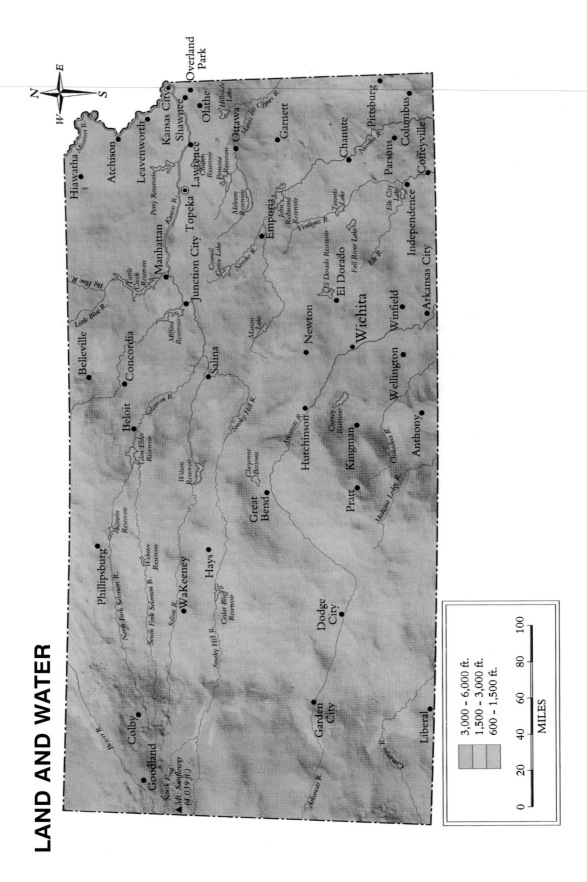

▨	3,000 – 6,000 ft.
▨	1,500 – 3,000 ft.
▨	600 – 1,500 ft.

MILES

0   20   40   60   80   100

The Ogallala Aquifer's water is being used at an enormous rate as Kansas's farmers irrigate their fields.

"We don't want to say 'no more,' but when the water is gone, it's gone. Farmers need to ask themselves, 'Is the value of the crop worth bringing up the water?'"

EXTREME WEATHER

"Everybody says, 'If you don't like the weather, wait a minute!' Well, that's true. I once watched the temperature drop forty degrees in one afternoon," laughs one Lawrence resident. Temperatures in Kansas can range from frigid to broiling. As early as March and as late as October, it can be a blistering 100 degrees Fahrenheit. On the other hand, you could find yourself shivering in below-freezing weather in July.

Kansas has a continental climate, which means very hot summers and very cold winters. When the winter snows come, aided by blustery winds, it is frigid. "They have gates on the turnpike and they just close the road straight through to the Rockies," says a High Plains resident. In the swirling snows early homesteaders sometimes tied a rope between their house and barn, fearing that they might otherwise lose their way and freeze to death. Despite winter's hardships, it was the heat of summer that forced tens of thousands of Kansas pioneers off their farms. Summer's achingly long, hot days often came without rain. Droughts parched fields and shriveled crops. Defeated homesteaders returned east, the signs on their wagons reading "In God We Trusted—In Kansas We Busted." In the west the average annual rainfall can be as little as 16 inches, while the southeastern part of the state may get up to 40 inches of rain each year. In June of 2007 heavy rains caused some of the worst flooding southeastern Kansas had seen in decades. The rising waters of the Verdigris River broke through a levee, flooding the town of Coffeyville. A local oil refinery leaked more than 40,000 gallons of crude oil into the river, and emergency crews were called out to help with the massive cleanup effort.

Hold on to your hat. Kansas is one of the windiest states in the nation. With an average wind speed of 14 miles an hour, Dodge City tops the list of windiest cities in the United States.

Kansas is located in an area of the United States known as Tornado Alley. Warm winds carrying moisture from the Gulf of Mexico may collide over the region with chilling blasts from the Arctic. Year round, but especially in spring and fall, these weather fronts draw battle lines on the plains. A carefree, balmy day may suddenly be ripped apart by hail, lightning, and tornadoes.

TWISTER COUNTRY

The Wizard of Oz is fiction, of course, but the twister that whisks away Dorothy's house is a vivid example of the wild weather that can sweep through Kansas. On average, Kansas gets about forty-seven tornadoes each year, ranking it among the top tornado states in the United States. One of its deadliest tornadoes occurred on the night of May 25, 1955. A massive F5 tornado carved a half-mile path of destruction through the small town of Udall, southeast of Wichita. With wind speeds in excess of 260 miles per hour, the violent tornado killed 83 people, injured 270, and destroyed nearly every home and building in the city. More recently, in May of 2007, an F5 flattened almost every building in the town of Greensburg, in south-central Kansas (population: 1,500). Ten people died as the worst tornado since 1999 cut a path of destruction across the state. Kansas, Oklahoma, and Texas are at the greatest risk for tornadoes. However, these violent whirlwinds can occur anywhere in the United States.

Kansans are used to facing nature's challenges. Tornadoes, dust storms, floods, droughts, lightning, hail, and blizzards are all part of life in the Sunflower State. Even so, most of the time the weather in Kansas is quite pleasant. In most places the sun shines overhead in a crystal-clear, blue sky for more than two-thirds of the year!

Chapter Two

Settling the Heartland

The first humans arrived in Kansas about 13,000 years ago. These people, called Paleo-Indians, hunted large animals, such as the woolly mammoth, and gathered nuts, roots, and berries. They were nomadic people who moved around in search of food, carrying their belongings with them.

Later came another group of people known as the Mound Builders, because they buried their dead in large dirt mounds. They formed permanent villages of dwellings made with woven grass and poles. The Mound Builders were Kansas's first farmers. They planted corn and squash in their fields.

By the 1500s descendants of the Mound Builders, called the Wichita, along with the Pawnee, lived in Kansas. The Wichita used poles and grass "shingles" to construct cone-shaped lodges, while the Pawnee made lodges of earth and compressed grasses. Women tended fields of corn and other crops, while the men hunted. Their most valued prey was the bison, or buffalo. When on the hunting trail, they lived in tepees made of buffalo skins. This way of life was similar to that of the Kaw and Osage peoples, who later moved into eastern Kansas. The Plains Apache

During the mid-1800s homesteaders flocked to Kansas to claim land. This is Witchita's Main Street in 1870.

followed herds of buffalo across western Kansas. In the 1700s the Comanche moved onto the Plains Apache territory. The Comanche raided the settlements of other groups. They were the most feared of all native peoples because they rode horses, making them swifter and more powerful than warriors on foot.

Horses played a large part in Comanche culture. This painting depicts the way they aided in the buffalo hunt.

THE HAWK AND HIS FOUR DOGS

The Wichita tamed dogs to help with hunting and farm chores. Many of their legends, like this one, honor their dogs:

Once a chief's son had four dogs: one white, one red, one black, one copper. He kept them tied near his grass lodge. The boy had special powers, and the dogs were his guardians. One day the boy went out walking. He met two beautiful women wearing buffalo-hide robes. They traveled together until they approached a herd of buffalo. Then suddenly the women transformed into buffalo and began attacking the boy.

The boy tried to use his special powers to escape the snorting and stamping Buffalo-Women. He called upon other creatures such as the eagle to help him escape, but they could not help.

Back at home his loyal dogs began barking furiously. The boy had asked his parents to unleash the dogs if they ever began barking. So the chief and his wife cut the ropes from the dogs' necks. The dogs raced to the boy's rescue and chased the buffalo away. However, the four faithful animals never returned home. Saddened by the loss of their companions and fearful of living without their protection, the boy and his family became hawks and flew away.

EUROPEANS ARRIVE

In 1541 the first Europeans found their way to Kansas. Spanish explorers from Mexico had been traveling north in search of a legendary kingdom of gold. In present-day New Mexico an American-Indian slave called El Turco, who hoped to return to his home in the Central Plains, convinced explorer Francisco Vásquez de Coronado that he knew where to find such a kingdom. He called it Quivira. For forty-two days the Spaniards tramped across the High Plains, searching for Quivira. After thundering across the Arkansas River and confronting an encampment of Wichita Indians, Coronado realized that the Wichita did not dwell in a city of gold. Disappointed, he turned back.

Soon other Spanish explorers and missionaries ventured into the area. In 1673 the first French explorers arrived from Canada. Interested in furs, they

Spanish explorer Francisco Vásquez de Coronado crosses the plains of Kansas while looking for a kingdom of gold.

discovered beaver and bison and began trading with the Osage and Pawnee. For more than one hundred years Spain and France fought over Kansas. Finally, in 1803, President Thomas Jefferson persuaded France to sell its land west of the Mississippi River, including Kansas, to the United States. The sale was called the Louisiana Purchase, and it doubled the size of the nation.

GO WEST, AMERICANS!

Many Americans living on the East Coast did not care about the western frontier. A Boston newspaper reported it to be "a waste, a wilderness unpeopled by anything but wolves and wandering Indians." Jefferson disagreed. He commissioned the Corps of Discovery, led by Meriwether Lewis and William Clark, to collect information about the new territory and

Members of the Lewis and Clark Expedition greet American Indians while exploring the Louisiana Territory.

its people. In 1804 they set out from St. Louis, Missouri, bound for the Pacific Ocean. Although their stay in Kansas was brief, they recorded news of "beautiful plains that were breathtaking." Two years later, Lieutenant Zebulon Pike was sent to the central and southern Great Plains to explore and keep peace with the Indians. Pike reported, "These vast plains of the western hemisphere may become in time as celebrated as the sandy deserts of Africa."

Pike's report influenced mapmakers to label the Great Plains "the Great American Desert." Later, U.S. Secretary of War John C. Calhoun used this information to determine that Kansas was "unfit for cultivation." He thought it would be a good place to relocate American Indians living in the East, where white settlers had been clamoring for more land. So, in 1830, Congress passed the Indian Removal Act, which forced twenty-seven eastern tribes west into what would become Kansas. The government declared the area that eventually would become Kansas part of the "permanent Indian frontier."

But it was not permanent. White settlers continued advancing on the frontier. The Santa Fe Trail, stretching from Franklin, Missouri, to Santa Fe, in what is now New Mexico, was a major trading route running across Kansas. The Oregon Trail passed through Kansas's northeastern corner. And when gold was discovered in California in 1848, thousands of hopeful prospectors

Part of the Santa Fe Trail passed through Council Grove, Kansas.

traversed Kansas on the Overland Trail. Between gold seekers, traders, and pioneers, more and more white settlers encountered Kansas. Some noted that the soil was actually very fertile. They demanded that the region be opened to homesteading. In 1854 the government passed the Kansas-Nebraska Act, permitting whites to settle in Kansas.

BLEEDING KANSAS

The Kansas-Nebraska Act made way for more than homesteading. It also opened the door to bloodshed and bitter rivalry. The act declared that Kansas had to choose whether or not to allow slavery. At the time Congress had as many members from Southern slave states as it did from Northern free states, and sessions often ended in deadlock. Each side wanted Kansas to vote with it. Proslavery groups, often called Bushwhackers, and abolitionists, sometimes called Jayhawks, fought viciously in Kansas. To thwart the Free State movement, Bushwhackers crossed into Kansas from Missouri and voted illegally for proslavery candidates who then passed proslavery laws. When abolitionists heard of this, hundreds migrated to Kansas to fight back. One of the most fanatical was John Brown. Abolitionists were usually nonviolent, but John Brown had seen enough. He and his sons led raids on proslavery settlements. Until he was hanged for leading a slave rebellion in 1859, Brown fought to free slaves. Violence so ruled Kansas during this period that it became known as Bleeding Kansas.

Kansas finally entered the Union as a free state on January 29, 1861. But that did not mean the bloodshed was over. The Civil War erupted almost three months later. By the time the Confederates surrendered in 1865, more than 20,000 Kansans had served in the Union army—more in proportion to population than any other state.

AN AMERICAN TRAGEDY

William C. Quantrill ("Quantrell") was a Confederate raider. A cold-hearted killer, he and his "border bandits," including outlaws Jesse and Frank James and Cole Younger, wreaked havoc during the Civil War. On August 21, 1863, after sacking several small towns along the Kansas-Missouri border, they rode into Lawrence, where they burned down some two hundred buildings and killed more than 150 residents. It was one of the largest civilian massacres ever in the United States.

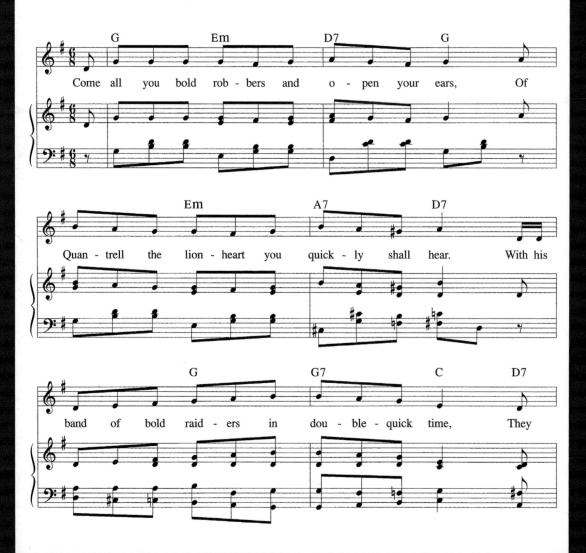

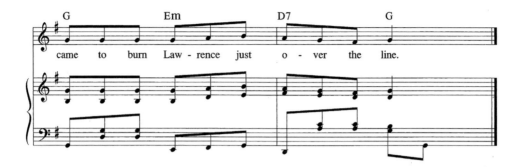

came   to   burn   Law - rence   just   o - ver   the   line.

Chorus:
All routing and shouting
And giving the yell,
Like so many demons
Just raised up from Hell,
The boys they were drunken
With powder and wine,
And came to burn Lawrence
Just over the line.

They came to burn Lawrence, they came not to stay,
They rode in one morning at breaking of day.
Their guns were a-waving and horses a-foam,
And Quantrell was riding his famous big road. *Chorus*

They came to burn Lawrence, they came not to stay,
Jim Lane he was up at the break of the day.
He saw them a-coming and got in a fright,
Then crawled in a corncrib to get out of sight. *Chorus*

FRONTIER LIFE

After the Civil War Americans resumed their westward expansion. For a ten-dollar fee any citizen could claim 160 acres of land. Thousands of veterans and freed slaves arrived in Kansas to stake their claims. Despite the hardships and uncertainties the homesteaders believed the West was the land of opportunity.

Pioneers first found shelter in crude tents or in their wagons. However, once they suffered their first Kansas storm, they realized a sturdy house was a necessity. Watching their plows churn up long, hard chunks of earth, they found a solution. By chopping the earth, or sod, into blocks, they could build a sod house, or soddy. For the roof they often used topsoil. You could guess how long a soddy had been standing by the height of the wild grass and

Sod houses, or soddies, like this one were constructed by Kansas's pioneers.

sunflowers that sprouted on the roof. Some soddies were simply a single wall in front of a dwelling carved into the side of a hill. This type was quicker to build but was more dangerous because sometimes a stray steer would wander across the roof and crash through onto the family below! Soddies were everywhere. Leaky and cold in winter and rodent-infested year-round, they were still beloved by grateful pioneers. Of her soddy, pioneer Lydie Lyons wrote, "The wind whistled through the walls in winter and the dust blew in summer, but we papered the walls with newspapers and made rag carpets for the floor, and we thought we were living well."

TRUE GRIT

Pioneer families homesteading in Kansas had to work as a team to survive. Men and women shared in the enormous challenges of conquering the prairie. Esther Clark's parents were pioneers. In her diary Clark writes about the strength of her mother, Allena:

Mother has always been the gamest one of us. I can remember her hanging onto the reins of a runaway mule team, her black hair tumbling out of its pins and over her shoulders, her face set and white while one small girl clung with chattering teeth to the sides of the rocking wagon and a baby sister bounced about on the floor in paralyzed wonder. But, I think, as much courage as it took to hang onto the reins that day, it took more to live twenty-four hours at a time, month in and month out, on the lonely and lovely prairie, without giving up.

The prairie wind was responsible for another common sight on the Kansas frontier, the windmill. It was a rare homestead that could boast a pond, stream, or river nearby, so pioneers dug deep wells for water. The pumps bringing water to the surface were powered by windmills.

WILD AND WOOLLY

In the 1860s the railroads surged westward. Tracks were laid from one end of Kansas to the other, changing the prairie forever. The first to suffer were the bison. For thousands of years Plains Indians had coexisted with their prey. Native people respected the bison, which they depended on for

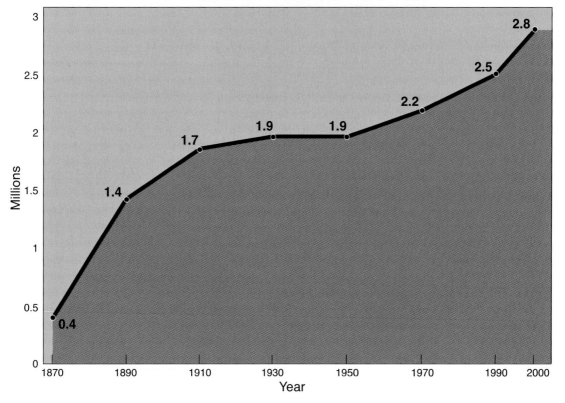

POPULATION GROWTH: 1870–2000

their livelihood. When they killed, they wasted nothing. They used the bison's flesh, skin, and bones for meat, fuel, shelter, clothing, blankets, weapons, and utensils. But when the whites killed, they did so only for food or sport. The railroads hired professional bison hunters, like "Buffalo" Bill Cody, to supply their crews with food. A single white hunter could bring down 250 animals a day. And no sooner were the railroads complete than thrill seekers hopped on board and took advantage of the easy targets. With guns aimed out windows, sport hunters shot into herds of bison, leaving the carcasses to rot along the tracks. Before white settlement 30 million bison roamed the plains. By 1890 they were nearly extinct. Without the buffalo to sustain them, the area's American Indians began to starve. The Indians who had not already been displaced by the U.S. government started leaving Kansas for reservation lands in Oklahoma and Texas.

In the late nineteenth century men would shoot buffalo for sport from moving trains, greatly reducing the buffalo population.

BRINGING BACK THE BISON

In the late 1880s federal laws were enacted to protect the bison of the Great Plains, but by then, only a few hundred animals remained. Thanks to conservation groups and ranchers who stepped forward in the twentieth century, the bison population slowly began to increase. Today thousands of bison graze on privately owned and protected land, like Smoky Valley Ranch in northwestern Kansas. Owned by the Nature Conservancy, the 16,800-acre preserve is helping to ensure the majestic bison remain part of the Kansas landscape well into the future.

Meat was scarce in eastern cities after the Civil War, but millions of wild longhorn cattle roamed Texas. Once railroads were built as far west as Kansas, cattle could be shipped to eastern markets. Cowboys in Texas rounded up the longhorns and drove them up the Shawnee, Chisholm, and Western trails to depots and stockyards in Baxter Springs, Abilene, Dodge City, Wichita, Ellsworth, and the like. Money and men poured in. Almost overnight the Kansas "cow towns" became boomtowns. Drawn by the lure of adventure, men and boys came from all over the country to become cowboys. Cattle drives were dusty, lonely, and treacherous, but once the cowboys brought the cattle to market, rowdy celebrations erupted. One journalist in Ellsworth reported, "Here you see in the streets men from every state and from almost every nation—the tall, long-haired Texas herder with his heavy jingling spurs and pair of six shooters; the gambler from all parts of the country, looking for unsuspecting prey; the honest immigrant in search of a homestead in the great free [W]est; the keen stockbuyers; the wealthy Texas drovers; deadbeats; pickpockets; and horse thieves."

The rough-and-tumble lawlessness of Kansas cow towns produced some of the West's most famous lawmen and gunfighters. Wild Bill Hickok, Wyatt Earp, Bat Masterson, and Doc Holliday were all Kansas gunslingers.

Cowboys drive cattle from Texas to Kansas on the Chisholm Trail.

THE REAL WILD WEST

"We're real Wild West!" declares Kansas historian Barbara Brackman. "Think about all the images Hollywood has created about the West. Outlaws, cattle drives, cowboys, Pony Express riders, gunslingers, frontier forts . . . they all belong to Kansas!"

Look at a map of Kansas and read the famous trail names: Chisholm, Oregon, Overland, Shawnee, and Santa Fe. When the cowboys rode into town to sell their cattle, buy supplies, and whoop and holler, where did they go? Abilene, Ellsworth, Cimarron, Wichita, and Dodge City. Think of the historic forts: Hays, Riley, Larned, Scott, and Leavenworth. There were also many legendary lawmen who kept the peace: Wyatt Earp, marshall of Wichita and Dodge City; Bat Masterson, Ford County sheriff; Wild Bill Hickok, marshall of Abilene; and Doc Holliday, dentist and deputy in Dodge City. And surely you have heard of Buffalo Bill Cody, the Pony Express rider, buffalo hunter, and Wild West Show promoter from Leavenworth, and Nat Love, known as Deadwood Dick, the African-American cowboy from Dodge City? Last, think of all the infamous bad guys who attacked unsuspecting Kansans: the Dalton, James, and Younger gangs, Quantrill's Raiders, and John Wesley Hardin. Also, nothing symbolizes the rugged American West quite like cowboy boots. And where were they made? Kansas, of course. "All the cowboys wanted to get their boots in Dodge City or Abilene," says Brackman. "They still make the best ones in Olathe, Kansas, the Cowboy Boot Capital of the World!"

"Barbed wire tamed the West," says one Kansas historian. Since the region had few trees, fences were rare. Although the longhorns ate well on the open range, their meat was stringy, and ranchers wanted to raise tastier breeds. But without fences they could not corral their herds. Then, in the 1870s, barbed wire was invented. Using the twisted lengths of sharp metal, ranchers could section off grassland cheaply and rein in their valuable livestock.

As new breeds of cattle were developed, new crops were grown to feed them. The Mennonites, a religious group that immigrated to Kansas from Russia, brought with them a remarkable variety of wheat called Turkey Red. Unlike other grains this was a winter wheat that was planted in the fall and harvested in the spring, before the harsh, dry summer set in.

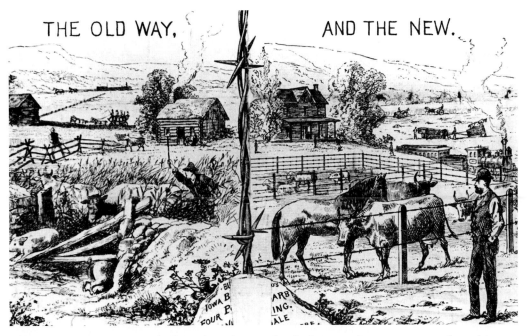

This illustration shows the benefits of using barbed wire, the new material used in fence construction in the 1870s.

Turkey Red thrived in Kansas. Flour mills were built, and Kansas's farmers and ranchers began changing their state's nickname from the Great American Desert to America's Breadbasket.

Dependence on ranching and farming meant living at the mercy of ever-unpredictable Mother Nature. Kansas farmers lived through cycles of boom and bust. The 1870s brought good rains and harvests but also a plague of locusts. Grasshoppers and locusts are closely related. Grasshoppers are harmless and solitary, and they stick close to home. But every once in a while, they use up their food supply, become excited, develop wings, and swarm. Once they are able to fly long distances, they are called locusts. A swarm of locusts sometimes covers 15 square miles! In 1874 the locusts came, stunning the pioneers. One homesteader wrote that the swarm was "so thick

Kansas farmers fight a locust plague.

you couldn't see the sun." Pioneer women watched in astonishment as the hoppers ate the wash on their clothes lines and the boards off their houses. One looked on in horror as "the hoppers came inside, eating all the food in the cupboards, the tool handles and furniture." The locusts' dying bodies poisoned the water; the air was filled with their smell. Chickens and hogs that ate the bodies tasted so much like the hoppers, they couldn't be eaten. Kansas's state government set up a relief committee for the victims of the plague and nearly went bankrupt trying to help them. But the worst was yet to come.

DEPRESSION AND WARS

When the United States entered World War I, in 1917, Kansans rallied in support of their country. Their battle cry was "Win the War with Wheat!" Tractors and plows turned more and more buffalo grass into cropland. Schoolchildren were encouraged to help farmers at harvest time. The army trained soldiers at Fort Riley's Camp Funston and at Fort Leavenworth. People sacrificed by having "meatless Tuesdays" and "wheatless Wednesdays." Kansas was feeding the world and mining coal, oil, and helium in an all-out war effort.

After the war the 1920s saw trucks, tractors, and combines replace plows and horses in the fields. Electricity was starting to reach rural areas, and everyone seemed to be buying Henry Ford's automobile. People were happy with their new mobility. For $295 you could buy a car and drive up to 40 miles an hour! Kansas oil fields grew richer as the automobile grew more popular.

But by the end of the decade, trouble was brewing. The stock market crashed in 1929, throwing the country into the Great Depression. Many people lost everything they owned. Wealth in land and wheat kept the Kansas economy from falling as hard and as fast as that of the rest of the country. When the state finally came undone, it was not from bad investments but largely because of nature. Four rainless years in the early 1930s dried up all the moisture in the ground throughout the southern Great Plains. So much grassland had been plowed under during the war effort that little vegetation remained to hold the remaining soil in place. In some places as much as 3 to 4 inches of topsoil was blown away. In Kansas, Oklahoma, Texas, New Mexico, and Colorado the dirt swirled in what people called black blizzards. The powdery soil collected against buildings and covered roads. During one rare shower the air was so full of dirt that it rained mudballs. Their livelihood gone with the wind, thousands of farmers left Kansas during what became known as the Dust Bowl. Those who stayed needed help from the government to survive.

In 1941 the country again went to war. Recruits from all over the nation were trained at army and navy bases in Kansas. Metal manufacturing,

A Kansas farmer attempts to work a field during the Dust Bowl.

aircraft production, and bumper crops of soybeans and grains were some of the contributions made by the state's hardworking men and women. The Boeing Company's aircraft manufacturing plant in Wichita was turning out four B-29 bombers a day! During the war Boeing Wichita built almost half of all the training aircraft used by the army and navy.

While news of World War II battles crackled over every radio, it was General Dwight D. Eisenhower, a Kansas farmboy, who led the armed forces in Europe. When he returned home to Abilene after the war,

B-29 bombers were constructed during World War II in Wichita.

he found a state brimming with renewed hope. Kansas was building dams to prevent floods; new agricultural methods were being used; music, theater, and other arts were blooming. Said the general, "The proudest thing I can say today is that I'm from Abilene." In the fall of 1952 Americans put their confidence in Eisenhower once again, electing the general from the thirty-fourth state to be the thirty-fourth president of the United States.

CIVIL RIGHTS AND SOCIAL CHANGE

Americans came home from the war and turned toward building a strong economy and a healthy society. Some Kansans were involved in one of the most significant events of the period. In 1951, eight-year-old Linda Brown lived in a racially mixed Topeka neighborhood. To get to school, Linda's white neighbors walked a few pleasant blocks to Sumner Elementary. But Linda and her African-American neighbors had to walk almost two miles from their home, crossing Topeka's busiest streets and a large railroad yard, in order to attend Monroe Elementary, a school for students who were not white. Linda's father and twelve other parents sued the Topeka Board of Education for not allowing their children to attend the closer school. Similar cases were also being brought before the courts in Delaware, Virginia, South Carolina, and the District of Columbia. These were combined with Brown's to become one federal case, *Brown vs. Board of Education*. Thurgood Marshall, who later became the first African-American U.S. Supreme Court justice, was the chief counsel for Linda Brown and the other African-American students. He argued that having separate, or segregated, schools for different races violated the Fourteenth Amendment to the Constitution, which guarantees all citizens "equal protection under the laws." In 1954 the U.S. Supreme Court ruled in a landmark decision that "education . . . is a right which must be made available to all. . . . Separate educational facilities are inherently [by nature] unequal." Linda Brown's family and neighbors had helped change the course of history. Segregation in schools was declared unconstitutional.

African Americans were not the only ones fighting for civil rights. War, starvation, disease, and displacement had taken a huge toll on the American-Indian population in the United States. In little more than a century many tribes of the Great Plains went from having tens of thousands of members to a few thousand or less. Worse, from the 1950s to the 1970s, the U.S. government tried to end "federal recognition" of numerous tribes. Without such recognition, America's Indian tribes could not receive federal funds for economic development, education, or health care. They also could not lay claim to ancient tribal lands. American Indians fought back by protesting and going to court. For some the battle to regain their rights stretched on for years. For others it is still ongoing. Today more than 550 national tribes have received federal recognition, including Oklahoma's Wichita, Kaw, Osage, and Comanche nations—groups that once thrived in pre-European Kansas. Northeastern Kansas is now home to four recognized Indian reservations: the Iowa, the Kickapoo, the Potawatomi, and the Sac and Fox.

The late twentieth century brought other social concerns to light in Kansas, such as mental health, prison reform, drug dependency, and child abuse. In 1980 Kansas became the first state in the United States to set up a fund to help stop child abuse and neglect. The Children's Trust Fund was a model for the rest of the nation, and today all fifty states have similar child abuse–prevention programs.

As the twenty-first century unfolds, lack of access to affordable health care, domestic violence, and poverty are some of the major social concerns facing the state. Kansans will no doubt tackle these issues with the same strength, spirit, and determination they have shown throughout their rich history.

Chapter Three

Under One Big Sky

In 2008 an independent research firm ranked Kansas as the seventeenth "Most Livable State" in the United States. The study took into account forty-four factors, such as crime rate, education, job growth, income levels, and traffic deaths. It even considered the percentage of sunny days each year (in Wichita, about 60 percent of the days are partly sunny or sunny)!

More than 2.7 million people call Kansas home. There are about thirty-three people per square mile in Kansas; that is much less than the national average of about eighty people per square mile. Even so, it is a misconception to think that everyone in Kansas lives on a farm. Most people live in or near Kansas City, Lawrence, Overland Park, Topeka, or Wichita. These urban centers offer all the cultural activities and high energy of any thriving American city.

Although 70 percent of Kansans are urban dwellers, they are never totally removed from nature and agriculture. Even racing along the interstate through Kansas City or Topeka, drivers can hear crickets chirping above the sounds of traffic. Wild sunflowers bloom along the roadways in summer while turkey vultures circle overhead. Road signs remind travelers, "Every Kansas farmer feeds 128 people and YOU!"

A truckload of harvested wheat becomes a play area for this Kansas boy.

CELEBRATIONS ON THE PLAINS

The population of early Kansas contained a mixture of European cultures. Germans, Swedes, Swiss, Russians, Czechs, English, Scots, and Irish were told by the railroads, which advertised all over northern Europe, that inexpensive farmland was available in Kansas. The towns these immigrants settled and the holidays they still celebrate highlight their beginnings. Among the observances are the Swedish Saint Lucia Day in Lindsborg and Victoria Days, a Catholic German celebration held near the Cathedral of the Plains, a mammoth limestone church in north-central Kansas.

Swedish folk dancers celebrate their heritage and culture at the Saint Lucia Day Festival in Lindsborg.

FLIPPING OVER PANCAKE DAY

Each February residents of Liberal, Kansas, and thousands of tourists come out for the traditional celebration of Pancake Day. "It's a very unique festival," says Liberal's Rosalee Phillips. The tradition goes back to 1445 in Olney, England. One morning a woman was making pancakes when she heard the church bells ring. In her haste to get to church, she dashed out of the house still wearing her headscarf and apron. She arrived on time, skillet in hand. And so Olney's Pancake Race was born. About five hundred years later the citizens of Liberal proposed an international competition. Women in Olney and Liberal run a 415-yard, S-shaped course wearing dresses, aprons, and headscarves while carrying a skillet containing a pancake. They have to flip the pancake at the start and at the finish. Three runners share a race record of 58.1 seconds.

Reports Phillips, "It's an all-out sprint, but if they cross the finish line without that pancake, they're out of the race! I always encourage the ladies to keep their thumb on it!"

Opposed to slavery and war and believing in leading a simple, charitable life, many Mennonites fled Russia in the 1870s, when Czar Alexander II insisted they join the army. Thousands of Mennonites came to the United States; ten thousand immigrated to Kansas. Many Kansans today share the Mennonite values of hard work and generosity. Every year at the Mennonite Relief Auction, handcrafted items, especially their world-famous quilts, are sold to benefit the poor.

Some of the Mennonites in Kansas are descendants of those who fled Russia during the 1870s.

One smaller Mennonite group, the Amish, settled near Yoder. Following stricter beliefs, the Amish live without electricity and farm much the way early pioneers did. "Just look where the power lines don't go," says Yoder resident Kathryn Troyer. "That will be an Amish farm. Be careful driving, too; their horses and buggies go right down the middle of the road." Ask anyone in the state about Yoder, and eyes roll up as stomachs are patted. "Oh, Yoder," everyone says. "The food the Amish make is so good!"

1-2-3-4 CAKE

This traditional cake is a Kansas farm kitchen favorite.

1 cup butter, softened
1 teaspoon vanilla extract
1 cup milk
1 teaspoon salt
2 cups sugar
3 cups flour
4 teaspoons baking powder
4 eggs

Preheat oven to 350 degrees Fahrenheit.

Cream the butter and sugar until the mixture is fluffy. Add eggs one at a time, beating after each addition. Stir in vanilla. Beat until combined.

In another bowl sift flour, baking powder, and salt together. Stir a little of the flour mixture into the butter/sugar mixture. Then add a little milk to the butter/sugar mixture and stir. Repeat, taking turns stirring in flour and milk little by little, until everything is combined (about five turns). Pour batter into an 8" x 13" baking pan that has been greased and floured. Bake 25 to 30 minutes or until a toothpick inserted in the center comes out clean. Frost with your favorite icing!

ETHNIC KANSAS

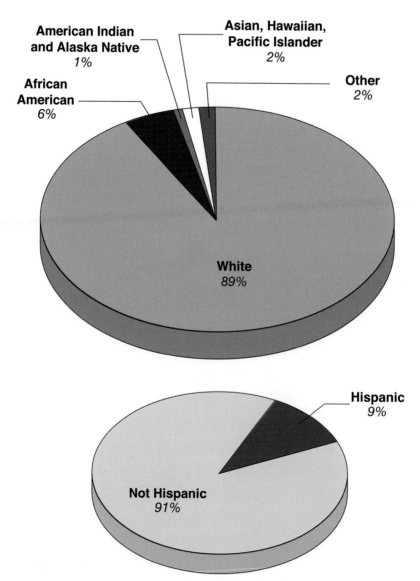

American Indian
and Alaska Native
1%

Asian, Hawaiian,
Pacific Islander
2%

African
American
6%

Other
2%

White
89%

Hispanic
9%

Not Hispanic
91%

*Note: A person of Cuban, Mexican, Puerto Rican, South or Central American,
or other Spanish culture or origin, regardless of race, is defined as Hispanic.*

In the early twentieth century, immigrants from Mexico began settling in Kansas. Today, at 9 percent of the state's population, Latinos are a well-established and growing group. Kansas City was recently voted among the top-ten places to live by *Hispanic* magazine. In Garden City the Mexican Fiesta held in September has been celebrated with parades, dances, and piñatas for more than seventy-five years. "It's huge," says one resident. "People come from all over the country."

Since the 1970s Southeast Asians from Cambodia, Laos, and Vietnam have been settling in Kansas. At that time meatpacking plants in rural areas were suffering a shortage of workers. Anxious to find work in their adopted country, Southeast Asians left California to fill the factory jobs in Kansas.

This Hispanic teen celebrates in the Fiesta Mexicana parade in Topeka.

Today 8 percent of the population of Garden City, in southwestern Kansas, is Southeast Asian. Shop signs are written in Vietnamese and Cambodian as well as in Spanish and English. Celebrations such as Tet, the Vietnamese New Year, have brought a rich and diverse atmosphere to the Old West.

About 6 percent of Kansans are African American, but you would never guess it from the number of people who attend "Homecoming" in the tiny town of Nicodemus. The town was homesteaded by ex-slaves following the Civil War and blossomed in the 1880s. But the High Plains were a harsh land, and the former slaves had few resources beyond their capacity for hard work, so when the railroad that was supposed to pass nearby was never built, the town faded. Today the town's population hovers around forty people, but "thousands of descendants from all over the country come to Homecoming," says a resident. "We have food, crafts, and a dance Friday and Saturday nights. There's a gospel extravaganza, church on Sunday with a community dinner afterward. Everybody brings something to share, and that's the way it's always been." In 1998 the town of Nicodemus became a national historic site.

Although more than twenty-five Indian groups have made their home in Kansas at one time or another, today less than 1 percent of Kansans is American Indian. Most native groups originally from Kansas now live in Oklahoma. One area where the American-Indian population is evident is in Lawrence, home of Haskell Indian Nations University, the only four-year American-Indian college in the country. The college has 800 students from 163 tribes. Ceremonies, powwows, and art markets are held on the school grounds, and the public is welcome to enjoy the displays of modern and traditional American-Indian life.

EXCELLENCE IN EDUCATION

Ensuring students get a good education is a priority in Kansas. The state devotes almost 40 percent of its budget to education, a greater percentage than in more populous states, including California and New York. Schools in the Sunflower State are among the best in the country. One magazine ranked Lawrence, Overland Park, and Shawnee Mission in the top 3 percent of metro areas in the United States for overall quality of education. Ninety percent of all students in Kansas get a high school diploma (the national average is 84 percent). More than two-thirds of the class of 2005–2006 went on to postsecondary education. And they had plenty of choices!

A story is read to a dual-language class in Dodge City.

The state has more than sixty private and public colleges and universities. Among the largest are Kansas State University, Wichita State University, and the University of Kansas (KU). KU in Lawrence was rated as one of America's Top National Universities in 2007 by *U.S. News & World Report*. It is also the alma mater of such famous names as former U.S. senator and presidential contender Bob Dole, National Basketball Association superstar Wilt Chamberlain, and National Football League Hall of Famer Gale Sayers.

Private four-year colleges include Friends University in Wichita, Bethany College in Lindsborg, and Winfield's Southwestern College. Baker University and Benedictine College, also private schools, were founded in eastern Kansas while the area was a still a territory. Established in Baldwin City in 1858, Baker is the oldest university in the state.

Prospective students discuss admissions options with a representative of Kansas State University.

POPULATION DENSITY

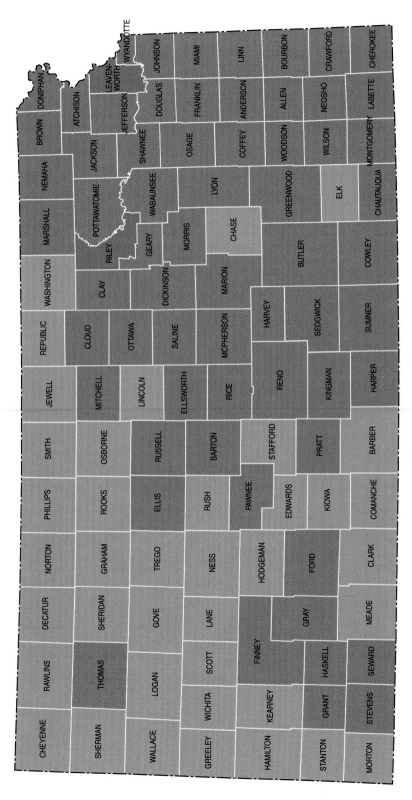

Persons per square mile

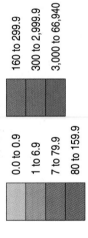

0.0 to 0.9	160 to 299.9
1 to 6.9	300 to 2,999.9
7 to 79.9	3,000 to 66,940
80 to 159.9	

CRIME AND PREVENTION

In 1992 Meade County, Kansas, reported zero crimes for the year. While the rest of the state cannot boast such a distinction, its crime rate is lower than the national average. "The key to control is prevention," says a Garden City police officer. "It's important how community police handle things. We have no tolerance for gangs." Adolescent drug and alcohol abuse prevention programs are very visible across the state.

Kansas has long fought against alcohol abuse. Many citizens from the late 1880s onward supported Prohibition, or the banning of liquor. Carry Nation of Medicine Lodge, Kansas, was famous for her activism. The widow of an alcoholic husband, she knew firsthand the curses of "Demon Rum." Brandishing a giant pickax, she slashed her way into saloons, demanding that the men stop drinking. Though she was arrested for her vandalism, many women followed her lead in fighting for Prohibition. In part because of their efforts, in 1920 the Eighteenth Amendment to the Constitution went into effect, prohibiting the manufacture and sale of alcohol. National Prohibition was short-lived. It ended in 1933 because legislators believed it was responsible for government corruption, gangs, and a higher crime rate. Despite the rest of the country's change of heart, Kansas did not repeal its state prohibition on alcohol until 1948. Today the state's alcohol consumption is less than half that of the national average. Carry Nation's influence lives on.

SMALL TOWN OR BIG CITY?

Although Dorothy in *The Wizard of Oz* tells us that "there's no place like home," not every Kansas citizen is as pleased as she. "There's nothing to do," complains one young Dodge City salesperson. "There used to be a college here and interesting people came to town. Now, there's [*sic*] two new meatpacking plants and the college closed. You have to go to Garden

The Jubilee parade takes place each year before the beginning of the wheat harvest in Lenora, Kansas.

City to do anything." In western Kansas the small cities that rely on cattle and oil are far removed from the diverse offerings of bigger cities. "We're six hours to Denver, four hours to Amarillo, Texas, and we're closer to Oklahoma City than Topeka," says Rosalee Phillips, longtime resident of Liberal. "We can always go to the big city but it's nice to live away from the hustle and bustle."

Sometimes young people who go away to college do not come back. It worries those who are content to live where there are no malls, streetlights, or movie theaters. "Some of our towns are really dying," says one Hodgeman County resident. But Jetmore's Nancy Ferguson-Moyer believes small-town life will always have its allure. Although many people move to the city for school or jobs, after they have families, the cities seem too intense; they want to come back home. "There's maybe only two houses for sale a year here, and they sell right away. We all want our backyards and our front yards and to be able to see the sky!"

In contrast to smaller, rural communities, most of the bigger cities in Kansas are thriving. Northeast Kansas is one of the fastest-growing metropolitan areas in the country. According to the U.S. Census

A HEALTHY STATE

In 2007 an independent research firm ranked Kansas as the tenth-healthiest state in the United States. The study took into account twenty-one key health factors, such as the number of adult smokers, obesity rates, immunization figures, access to health care, and even seat belt usage!

Bureau between the years 2000 and 2005 almost 60,000 people moved to Kansas, many relocating from more densely packed states like California and Massachusetts. Some are native Kansans who left in the 1980s and 1990s and have decided to come home. They are all coming to the Sunflower State for affordable housing, good schools, safe neighborhoods, tight-knit communities, clean air and water, and less traffic congestion.

Kansans can say they are from eastern Kansas or western Kansas. Or they can say they hail from the city or from the country. But no matter how they define themselves, Kansans generally agree on one thing—where they come from, people are friendly.

Chapter Four

Kansas Works

Kansas's state government is based in Topeka, which has served as the state capital since 1861. The Kansas Constitution is similar to the U.S. Constitution in that it divides government into three branches: executive, legislative, and judicial.

INSIDE STATE GOVERNMENT

Executive

The head of state in Kansas is the governor. He or she prepares the budget and approves or rejects proposed laws. Other elected executive-branch officials include the lieutenant governor, the secretary of state, and the attorney general. All executive officials serve four-year terms.

Legislative

The Kansas legislature is made up of a house of representatives and a senate. The house has 125 members elected to two-year terms. In the senate 40 members serve four-year terms. The legislature is elected by the people. Each house member represents about 19,000 Kansans, while each senator represents about 60,000 citizens. Once most members of both houses approve a

Kansas's state capitol is located in Topeka.

The Kansas Senate Chamber is known for being one of the most beautiful legislative rooms in the nation.

proposed law, or bill, it is sent to the governor. The governor may sign the bill into law or veto it, which makes the bill invalid.

Judicial

The Kansas court system is divided into a supreme court, a court of appeals, district courts, and municipal courts. The supreme court is the state's highest court. The decisions of the seven supreme court justices take precedence over those of all other courts. The governor selects supreme court justices from a list of nominees provided by a committee of lawyers. Once appointed, a justice must be reelected by voters every six years.

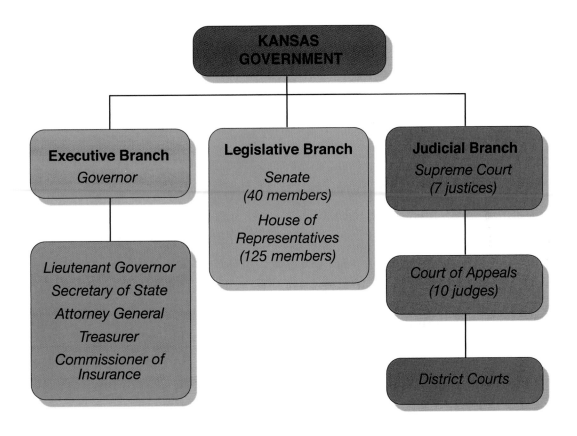

District courts hear most of the state's cases. Those who are dissatisfied with a district court ruling can ask for another trial. Most of these appeals are heard in the court of appeals, although some serious cases are heard by the supreme court. The supreme court can also review cases heard by the court of appeals. Municipal courts are city courts that handle minor crimes, such as traffic violations. But all judges have the same duty—to interpret laws made by the legislature and to apply the laws fairly.

County and local governments also play a key role in shaping daily life in Kansas. There are 105 counties in the state and more than 600 incorporated cities. In each county, voters go to the polls to choose a county commission, county attorney, clerk, sheriff, and other officials. Many towns also elect a mayor and city council to create laws, oversee the budget, and manage economic growth in their communities.

On the national level Kansas is represented in Congress by four members in the House and two senators. The state has six electoral votes in presidential elections.

WOMEN MAKE THEIR MARK

"Kansans are independent thinkers," says historian Barbara Brackman. In 1861, the year Kansas became a state, the very first legislature gave women the right to vote in school elections. By 1887 women were casting their ballots in local elections. As a result, women in Argonia, Kansas, voted for the first time alongside their brothers, husbands, fathers, and sons. They helped to elect Susanna Madora Salter the first female mayor in the country. Kansas women were allowed to vote in state elections by 1912, eight years before the Nineteenth Amendment to the U.S. Constitution gave women across the country the right to vote.

DID YOU KNOW?

While Kansas was still a territory, its capital was moved numerous times, depending on whether the ruling party was proslavery or antislavery. Fort Leavenworth, Shawnee Mission, Pawnee, Minneola, Lawrence, and Lecompton all served as the seat of territorial government at one time or another (some of them several times). The people finally selected Topeka to be the state capital when Kansas entered the Union. Here are a few fascinating facts about Kansas's capitol:

- It took thirty-seven years to finish construction on the Capitol (from 1866 to 1903), at a cost of $3.2 million.
- In the east wing you can see the famous 31-foot by 11-foot mural *Tragic Prelude* by John Steuart Curry. The painting features John Brown leading abolitionists in a fight against proslavery forces.
- It cost more than $140,000 to decorate the Senate Chamber. The imported French stained-glass windows, blue marble wall from Belgium, and twenty-eight bronze columns were seen as an extravagance during construction, but today the room is considered one of the most beautiful chambers in the United States.
- Within a year of the start of construction, the building's original sandstone foundation was crumbling (partly due to the harsh winters in Kansas) and had to be replaced.
- Today the Capitol is undergoing a $140 million refurbishing project to repair deteriorating stone and broken marble, restore historic paintings and murals, and update the building to handle modern technology.

In the 1990s Kansas broke ground again when it became the first state in the United States to have a female governor, Joan Finney; a female senator, Nancy Landon Kassebaum; and a female congressman, Jan Meyers—all serving at the same time. Kansans chose Kathleen Sebelius as their governor in 2002. She was reelected for a second term four years later. In 2006 Sebelius was named by *Time* magazine as one of the top-five governors in the country. She stood out as an example for her efforts to balance the budget while not increasing taxes or cutting funding for education. Sebelius is the first daughter of a U.S. governor, Ohio's John Gilligan (1971–1975), to serve in the same position—although for a different state.

Joan Finney was the nation's first female governor.

Kansas was also the first state in the Union to ratify the Fifteenth Amendment to the Constitution, which granted voting rights to African-American men.

HOG POLITICS

One issue dividing Kansans today is swine. "Hogs are hot around here," says one Great Bend resident. Actually, they are "hot" all around Kansas and the Midwest. Hog farms owned by large corporations have been moving into traditional family-farm areas. In Kansas it "has pitted neighbor against neighbor," says a waitress in Jetmore, "cousin against cousin!" A typical family hog farm may raise a few hundred hogs, but the corporate farms rear five to ten thousand hogs at once.

KANSAS BY COUNTY

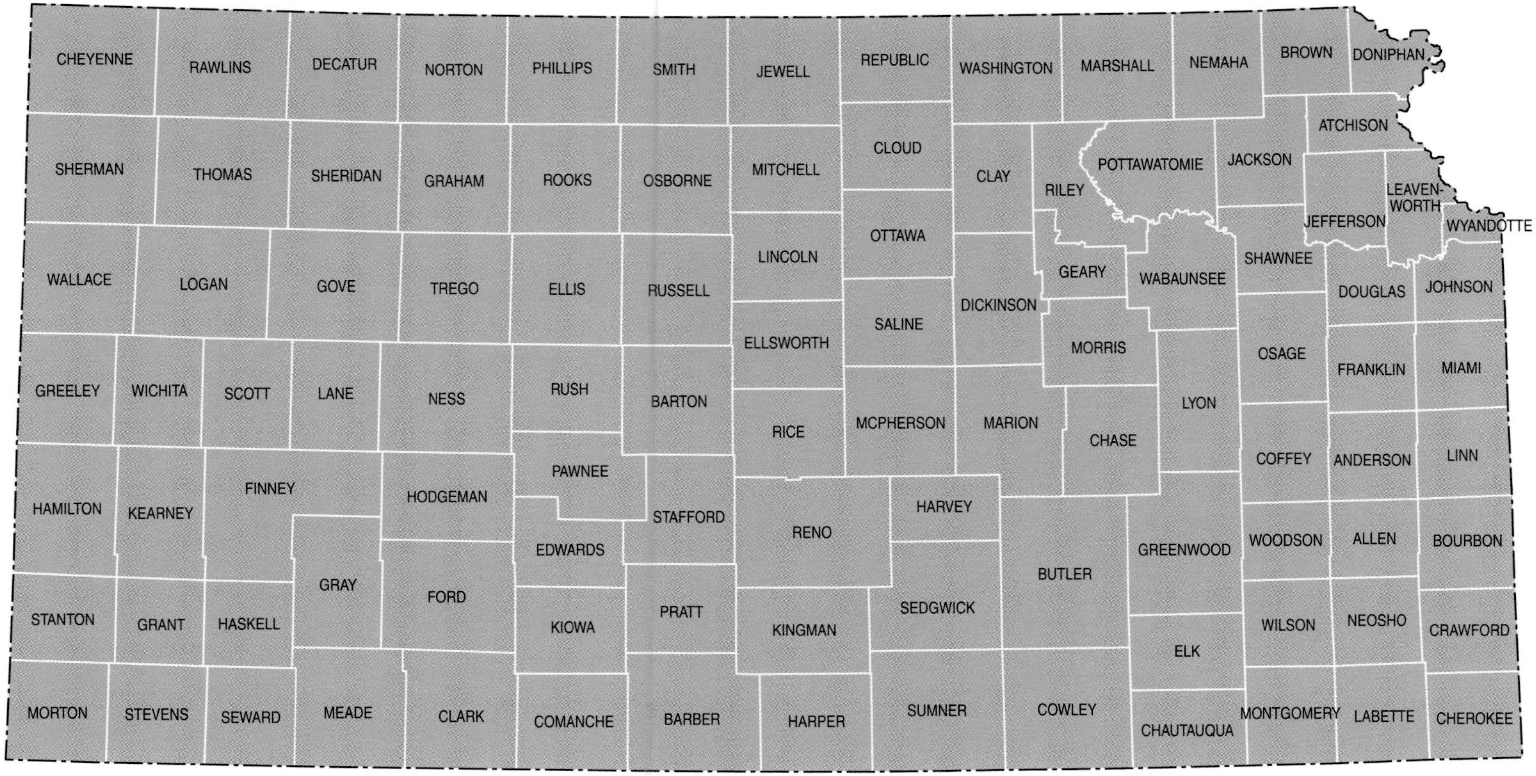

KANSAS QUIRKS

Most states have their share of wacky laws, and Kansas is no exception. Many of the following bits of legislation are outdated, some are weird, and others just do not make any sense at all:

- All businesses in Dodge City are required to have a horse water trough.
- Cars entering the city limits of Lawrence must honk to warn horses of their arrival.
- Anyone crossing a highway at night is required to wear taillights.
- It is illegal to ride an animal down the highway in Derby.
- It is against state law to shoot at rabbits from a motorboat.
- It was once illegal to serve ice cream on cherry pie in Kansas.
- State law requires that, if two trains meet on the same track, neither shall proceed until the other has passed.

People who welcome the corporate farms believe they will see more jobs and money coming into their towns. Opponents fear the environmental damage the pigs could cause. Bacteria-filled hog waste is stored in large lagoons, from which it can seep into the groundwater or flow into nearby streams. Odor is another serious concern. "Some corporations in other states haven't been good land stewards," says Al Silverstein of Great Bend. "We see their mistakes and say, 'How can we do it different?'" Silverstein advises, "Don't think of it as 'freaky environmentalists' versus mighty corporations, either. Environmentalists are very mainstream individuals these days.

Many of the hog farms in Kansas can raise more than five thousand hogs.

THE FARMERS' PARTY

According to writer Mark Twain, the 1880s and 1890s were a "time in America when the rich got richer and the poor, poorer." The railroads gouged farmers with high shipping fees on their crops, and banks charged high interest on loans. Farmers cried foul. First they joined the Grange and the Farmers' Alliance. Through these groups farmers tried to form a united front against low crop prices and unfair costs. Later they formed their own political party, the People's, or Populist, Party. Populists wanted protection from the railroads and banks. They accused the government of favoring rich corporations. The Populist Party got many important reforms passed, such as child labor laws, a shortened workday, and new banking laws. Twice in the 1890s Kansans elected populists to be their governor and, for a time, the party held control of the state legislature. However, failure to pass major railroad reforms, rising farm prices, and political divisions zapped the movement of its strength. By 1908 the Populist Party disbanded. Even so, many populist ideals, such as the eight-hour workday, survived.

Everybody wants good water quality, clean air, and to protect our land. Farmers care a great deal about protecting their soil. The land is their factory."

In Great Bend four city council members who supported the corporate hog industry were voted out of office. And in Jetmore, where bumper stickers proclaimed "People vote . . . Hogs don't," citizens voted not to allow a corporate hog farm to locate there. Controversy over the hog farms will likely continue for years.

The Kansas state motto is *Ad Astra per Aspera*, which means "to the stars through difficulties." One of the biggest difficulties facing modern Kansas politicians is balancing the needs of growing cities with those of struggling farming communities. Many smaller, dwindling towns in the west often feel frustrated when watching cities in the east receive economic perks, while they are barely staying afloat. Kansas is working to bridge the gap between east and west, urban and rural.

Chapter Five
Agriculture, Aviation, and Beyond

Kansans built their state on a foundation of agriculture. Although it is still a key industry, a more diverse economy supports the Sunflower State today. Farming and ranching, manufacturing, mining, retail sales, business, tourism, technology, and energy production contribute to the state's healthy job market (unemployment in Kansas is typically among the lowest in the nation). The state's central location is also a plus, attracting many national and international businesses to America's heartland. International exports are also playing a key role in Kansas's economic growth. In 2007 the state exported more than $10 billion in goods—a record high.

BOUNTIFUL HARVEST

Kansas is one of the nation's leading producers of wheat, grain sorghum, and beef. About 50 million acres in the Sunflower State are devoted to raising

The wheat grown in Kansas accounts for 20 percent of the nation's annual supply.

A ripening wheat field seems to go on forever in Salina.

crops or livestock—that's about 90 percent of the total land area. Kansas grows 20 percent of the nation's annual supply of wheat, which is why it is often referred to as the "breadbasket" of the United States. A train stretching from the Sunflower State to the Atlantic Ocean would be needed to hold all of the wheat grown in Kansas in a single year!

Kansas also ranks among the top states in the production of grain sorghum, alfalfa, barley, and soybeans. Sorghum is a grass-type plant. The grains, stalks, and leaves of some types of sorghum are used for cattle feed. Sweet sorghum is used to make molasses and syrups.

Livestock is big business in Kansas. With more than 6.5 million heads of cattle, the state's cattle population outnumbers the human population by two to one! In 2005 meatpacking plants processed almost 6 billion

There are more than 6 million head of cattle in Kansas.

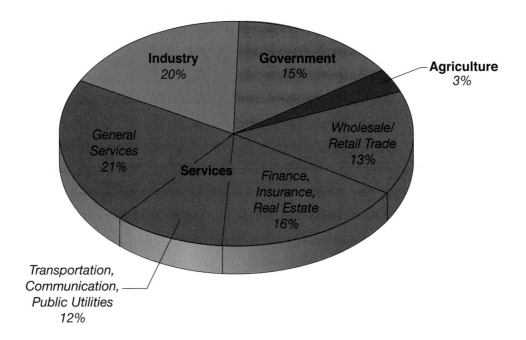

2006 GROSS STATE PRODUCT: $111 Million

- Industry 20%
- Government 15%
- Agriculture 3%
- Wholesale/Retail Trade 13%
- Finance, Insurance, Real Estate 16%
- Services
- General Services 21%
- Transportation, Communication, Public Utilities 12%

pounds of red meat. Food processing is one of the state's largest industries. One in five Kansans works in a job related to agriculture or food production. In 2005 cash receipts from farms in Kansas topped $10 billion, and exports of agricultural products were estimated at nearly $3 billion.

MANUFACTURING AND SERVICES

When you think of Kansas, you probably think of wheat, corn, or cattle. But as much as Kansas is a major supplier of these products, many more people head for jobs in the city than work on farms. Fewer than 10 percent of Kansas's workers are employed on farms. And it is expected that farms will employ even fewer people in the years to come. The fastest-growing job markets in the state are in manufacturing, construction, and services.

Wichita is often called the Air Capital of the World. As early as 1908 planes were being built in Kansas. Aviators from all over the world were attracted to the activity in Wichita. The uncluttered countryside was perfect for experiments with flight. It was an exciting time, though not everything was smooth sailing. After landing in a pasture, one pilot sent this telegraph message: "Motor cut. Forced landing. Hit cow. Cow died. Scared me." Cows today have little to fear from unexpected aircraft landings; they graze in safety far from the state's largest city.

More than 50 percent of the airplanes flown in the world today are made in Kansas. Wichita leads the nation in the production of business and military planes. More private aircraft are produced there than anywhere else on the planet. Boeing, Raytheon, Cessna, and Bombardier combined employ about 35,000 people in the area, making Wichita's aerospace industry the state's largest employer.

Employees at the Beechcraft factory assemble planes.

The Coleman Company, whose coolers keep our soda cold, got its start in 1900 renting oil lamps to miners. Today it employs thousands of Wichita workers. Pizza Hut also began in Wichita. In 1958 two college-aged brothers started their first restaurant with six hundred dollars they borrowed from their mother. Today company headquarters remain in Kansas while millions of their pizzas are sold around the globe. Many pizzas are ordered using telecommunications systems supplied by Sprint, whose world headquarters are near Kansas City. Nearby Hallmark Cards employs Kansans, as do railroads, hospitals, food-preparation plants, and car manufacturer General Motors. Payless Shoes, Cobalt Boats, Applebee's, and Goodyear Tire and Rubber Company are all based in Kansas. "We have so much going on," says one computer technician, "I wish people didn't just think of Kansas and wheat!"

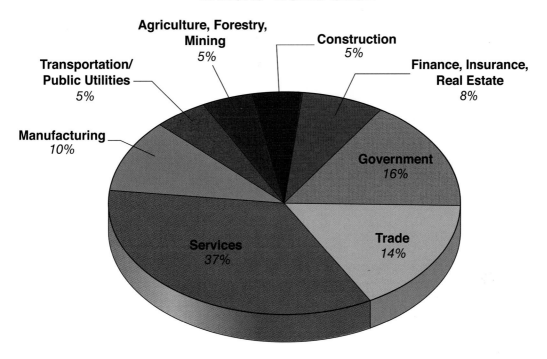

KANSAS WORKFORCE

Agriculture, Forestry, Mining 5%

Construction 5%

Transportation/Public Utilities 5%

Finance, Insurance, Real Estate 8%

Manufacturing 10%

Government 16%

Services 37%

Trade 14%

NATURAL RESOURCES

Mining plays a smaller role in the state's economy today than it once did. However, many oil and natural gas wells around the state are still pumping. The largest natural gas field in the nation is in southwestern Kansas, near Hugoton. Kansas is the nation's leading producer of helium, a gas used in balloons, underwater diving tanks, and computer semiconductors. Helium is mined in southeastern Kansas.

Coal, limestone, and salt are also mined in Kansas. The largest salt mine in the state, in Hutchinson, measures 650 feet deep and 43 football fields across. The mine has a surprising claim to fame: half a million boxes of important documents, microfilm, and other treasures are stored in the spaces

EARNING A LIVING

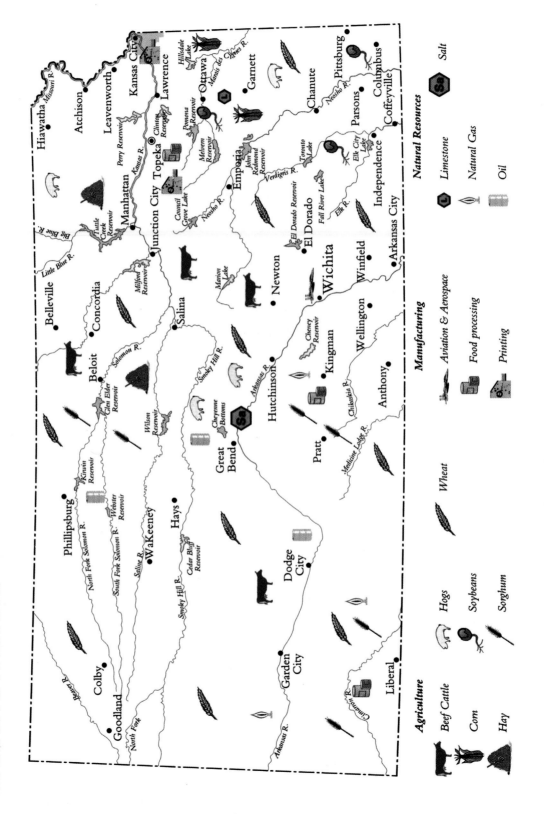

Natural Resources

Sn Salt

Limestone

Natural Gas

Oil

Manufacturing

Aviation & Aerospace

Food processing

Printing

Agriculture

Beef Cattle

Corn

Hay

Hogs

Soybeans

Sorghum

Wheat

where the salt has been excavated. At a constant sixty-eight degrees, the mine's environmental conditions are perfect for preserving these items. The vault is "a favorite with all the major Hollywood studios," says Lisa Rarick, who works for the Hutchinson Salt Mine. "Down in the mine, we have the original negatives of thousands of films. Some are priceless, like *The Wizard of Oz* and *Gone with the Wind*." Making a film archive out of a hole in the ground is just one more example of how Kansans turn the ordinary into the extraordinary.

WINDS OF CHANGE

The ever-present Kansas wind is proving to be a valuable source of renewable energy. In the 2000s several wind farms were built throughout the state, in Gray County, Spearville, and Elk River in the Flint Hills (though not without some controversy over their effect on the vanishing tallgrass prairie). In addition, nearly thirty other wind farm projects are on the drawing board. Kansas now ranks third in the nation for the production of wind power. The governor's goal is to have renewable energy produce 10 percent of the state's electricity by 2010 and 20 percent by the year 2020.

In the early 2000s Kansas began vying to become a center in the field of bioscience research and development. Bioscience is the study of the structure of living organisms, from microscopic cells to full-scale ecosystems, with the goal of engineering new products. Bioscience is useful in developing better medical equipment and devices, drugs, and crops. In 2004 the state created the Bioscience Authority, setting aside $580 million to invest in bioscience projects and companies in Kansas over a fifteen-year period.

Governor Kathleen Sebelius recently proposed creating the Office of Rural Opportunity. It will focus on attracting new businesses and families to areas of rural Kansas that are in desperate need of economic stimulus.

GOING GREEN WITH BIOFUELS

Most of the cars and trucks on U.S. highways run on petroleum, a nonrenewable energy source that contributes to air pollution, acid rain, and global warming. But Kansas is working to decrease America's dependence on fossils fuels through the production of biofuels.

Biofuels are made with organic matter such as corn, soybeans, or vegetable oil (they are usually mixed with fossil fuels). Biofuels are renewable and biodegradable, and they put out fewer pollutants than petroleum. The downside is that, when farmers focus on producing crops for fuel rather than food, prices may rise at the grocery store.

Ethanol, a type of biofuel made with corn, barley, or wheat, is already being produced in eight plants in Kansas (eighteen more plants are proposed). Many Kansans see the future of biofuels as a win-win proposition. New plants provide jobs and pump dollars into sagging rural areas, while the biofuels they produce give Americans a "greener" choice at the pumps.

Governor Sebelius is confident it can succeed. "If Cobalt Boats can dominate the market from Neodesha, or ABZ Valves can be a worldwide presence from its headquarters in Madison," she said, "there's no reason the next global leader in technology, energy or biosciences can't be founded in rural Kansas."

VACATION DESTINATION

Fun is proving to be quite profitable in the Sunflower State. Tourism in Kansas is a $5.6 billion a year industry. From across the Heartland and the nation visitors travel to the state to do all kinds of things: stroll through Wichita's botanical gardens, soak up the beauty of the Flint Hills, discover one or two (or more!) of the nation's top aviation museums, explore dusty cow towns steeped in legends of the Old West.

According to the Kansas Travel Industry Association, tourists spend $260 million in the state each year. Their dollars not only boost the economy but also help create more than six thousand new jobs in the restaurant, hotel, retail, and amusement industries. Each year more than 20 million U.S. citizens visit the Kansas City metropolitan area, which includes Kansas City, Missouri, just across the state line. What are they doing? Shopping, dining, sightseeing, gaming, and attending sports events, to name a few.

Visitors enjoy a re-created pioneer town in Dodge City.

GOOD SPORTS

Kansans love their sports teams. Major League Soccer's Wizards are based in Kansas City. Fans of professional baseball and football only have to take a short drive across the state border (and the Missouri or Kansas River) to Kansas City, Missouri, to watch Major League Baseball's Royals and the Chiefs of the National Football League. College sports are also extremely popular. In 2008 the University of Kansas men's basketball team gave fans plenty to cheer about when they brought home the N.C.A.A. national championship. The Jayhawks beat the University of Memphis 75–68 in an overtime game. It was the team's fifth national title in the school's 142-year history and its first since 1988.

Museums, cultural and arts events, festivals, and fairs also bring in tourists. Perhaps nothing draws bigger crowds, pleases more people, or shows off the state better than the Kansas State Fair, held in Hutchinson each September. "September is our beautiful month," says Kansan Nade Dangerfield, "and the fair is a slice of life not to be missed." The wheat harvest in Kansas is in the spring, not autumn, but the state fair still displays Kansas's fruitful bounty. From the longest ear of corn (a recent winner was 11 inches) to 1,200 wheat entries, 400-pound pumpkins, and exhibits of quilts, flowers, toy robots, photography, computers for use in tractors, Watusi goats, llamas, ostriches, buffalo, milking barns, big-name rock stars, and pig races, there really is something to amuse just about everyone.

From the carnival rides to foods as diverse as Indian tacos and Amish sour cream raisin pie, a day at the fair is a memorable experience. New and very popular is the Kansas State University School of Veterinary Medicine's Birthing Center. Fairgoers can watch calves, piglets, and chicks being born and possibly have the chance to hold one of the newborns. Said one sixth-grade teacher from Wichita who brought his class to the birthing center, "It's really incredible! A great field trip!"

There is nothing better than an ear of roasted corn from the Kansas State Fair.

Chapter Six

See the Sunflower State

Did you know Kansas has more miles of public roads than all but three states? With 136,000 miles of highways, interstates, turnpikes, city streets, and rural byways, there are plenty of ways to explore the Sunflower State. Ready to see some stunning scenery, quirky roadside attractions, and rugged Wild West towns? Hop in, and let's hit the road!

NATURAL WONDERS

While traveling westward across Kansas, the rolling hills and farms give way to tallgrass prairie at Flint Hills. "I've lived everywhere," says Cassoday waitress and steer roper Debbie Hoy, "but I always come back to the Flint Hills. It's a place where everything happens. And the animals—we have badger, possum, fox, mink, bobcats, deer, skunk, 'coons, wild turkey, prairie chickens, coyote, and now even armadillos are moving up." Roam the Tallgrass Prairie National Preserve and see and hear the hundreds of species of birds, insects, wildflowers, reptiles, and other animals.

Natural Kansas is more than grasses. "You have to get out of your car and look," says biologist Nade Dangerfield. "The geology of Kansas is wild."

The Buffalo Soldier Monument honors the African-American soldiers who fought in the Civil War.

The Monument Rocks National Landmark formations near Oakley in western Kansas are giant towers of chalk filled with fossils from an ancient sea. Fossil remains of clams, oysters, sharks, fish, and flying reptiles can be found there. The nearby Fick Fossil and History Museum houses more than 11,000 sharks' teeth collected from the area. Not far down the road is Castle Rock, another chalk spire, which rises 70 feet straight up from the surrounding plain.

Near Ellsworth, in north-central Kansas, are the Mushroom Rocks. These huge sandstone formations look like orbs balanced on pedestals. Covering an area the size of two football fields, Rock City, outside of Minneapolis, consists of more than two hundred rocks, some as big as houses. They were important (and startling) trail markers for the pioneers heading west. Rock City has changed little since it was formed millions of years ago.

More than four thousand visitors come see the two hundred house-size rocks each year at Rock City.

MIGHTY BIG SUNFLOWERS

Kansans are used to seeing good-sized sunflowers, but a piece of artwork in Goodland in western Kansas (near the Colorado border) has taken the large flowers to a whole new level. It is hard to miss the 80-foot steel easel rising up from the prairie or the enormous painting of sunflowers perched on it. Aptly titled the *Big Easel Project,* the artwork is the creation of Canadian artist Cameron Cross. It is part of a series of giant reproductions of artist Vincent Van Gogh's seven famous sunflower paintings. Cross's other Van Gogh reproductions are on display in Canada, Australia, the Netherlands, Japan, South Africa, and Argentina. So just how big is the painting in Goodland? It is 24 feet by 32 feet high and weighs 3,200 pounds!

HITTING THE TRAIL

Kansas, by virtue of its central location, has long been a crossroads. Indians, explorers, traders, and settlers have traveled the length and breadth of the state, leaving behind their marks. Historic Kansas was covered in trails, and many modern roads follow those old trails.

Two towns along the Oregon Trail are particularly good stopovers. Atchison, the hometown of female aviation pioneer Amelia Earhart, has museums devoted to her life, but its most beautiful memorial to her is the Ninety-Nines' International Forest of Friendship. The Ninety-Nines is an organization of female pilots from around the world. Earhart was its first president. She once wrote, "You haven't really seen a tree until you've seen its shadow from the sky." With this in mind,

On July 26, 1997, a crowd gathered to celebrate the dedication of the Earhart Museum.

the Ninety-Nines built trails and gardens and planted trees representing all fifty states and dozens of countries. Stone markers honor pilots and astronauts such as Charles Lindbergh, Sally Ride, and the Wright brothers.

Also along the old Oregon Trail is Leavenworth, Kansas's first city. The town is distinguished by Fort Leavenworth, the oldest active-duty army fort west of the Mississippi River, which was first established to guard a military road through Indian Territory. Probably the most famous federal prison in the country is also in Leavenworth. Often called the Big House by lawbreakers, the massive building resembles the U.S. Capitol, complete with a silver dome on top. Architects designed the building to impress citizens with the grandeur of the law. Many notorious prisoners have called the Big House home, including gangsters Al Capone and Machine Gun Kelly, and the Bird Man of Alcatraz.

Fort Leavenworth's military prison dates back to the 1860s.

THE BUFFALO SOLDIERS

Fort Leavenworth has had many notable officers, including President Dwight D. Eisenhower and former Secretary of State Colin Powell. When General Powell was stationed at Leavenworth, he noticed that there was very little mention of the 9th and 10th cavalries.

These two regiments were composed of African-American soldiers who fought in the Civil War. Afterward many of them remained in the army. Because of their skin color, they were given the worst rations, horses, and assignments. They were ordered to protect settlers and stagecoaches from Indian raids, and despite their unfair treatment, they fought fiercely. Their loyalty and courage impressed even their main foes, the Cheyenne. The Cheyenne respected them so much that they called them the Buffalo Soldiers, after their tribe's greatest symbol of bravery, the buffalo. The 9th and 10th cavalries accepted the name as a badge of honor.

Powell wanted to call the nation's attention to the Buffalo Soldiers and all the other African-American soldiers who have served in the U.S. military. He urged the government to build a memorial. The Buffalo Soldier National Monument now stands in Leavenworth. When it was dedicated, in 1992, Powell declared that "the terrible overlooking of Black heroism in the military finally has ended."

The longest trail through Kansas was the Big Lonely, or the Santa Fe Trail, which stretched all the way across Kansas. Today Highway 50 follows the old trail. In places, wagon ruts are still visible. Soldiers at Fort Larned protected traders along the trail. A walk through its buildings provides a taste of life on the frontier. Nearby is the impressive limestone outcropping Pawnee Rock, where the Pawnee tribe held council meetings.

Looking nearly the same today as it did over a century ago, Council Grove is a lush river town brimming with a rich past. For many years the only trading post along the Santa Fe Trail, Council Grove was where travelers made last-minute repairs or gathered final supplies. The Osage and Kaw tribes signed a treaty with the U.S. government allowing the Santa Fe Trail to cross their lands. The treaty was signed under a tree known as the Council Oak. That tree still stands. So does the Post Office Oak, a tree with a large knothole where trail riders left each other mail.

The Madonna of the Trail statue in Council Grove honors the women who crossed the country on the Santa Fe Trail.

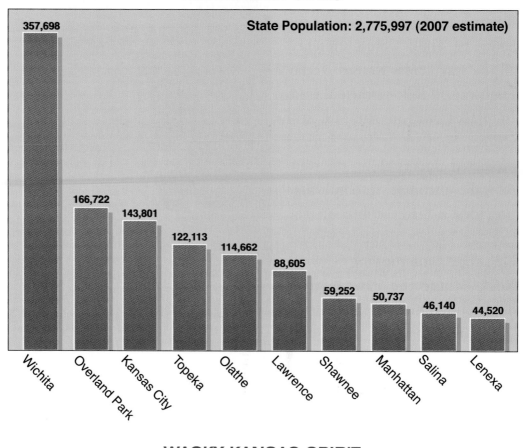

TEN LARGEST CITIES

State Population: 2,775,997 (2007 estimate)

- Wichita: 357,698
- Overland Park: 166,722
- Kansas City: 143,801
- Topeka: 122,113
- Olathe: 114,662
- Lawrence: 88,605
- Shawnee: 59,252
- Manhattan: 50,737
- Salina: 46,140
- Lenexa: 44,520

WACKY KANSAS SPIRIT

Visitors touring Kansas cannot help but come face to face with the unexpected. "It's the wacky Kansas spirit," says historian Barbara Brackman. It can appear anywhere, at any time.

For instance, what would you do with a big hunk of outdated machinery? You would build a park around it, of course! At least, that's what the people of West Mineral decided to do. Driving through the heart of Kansas's mining country, you will see a mountain of steel looming on the horizon. This is "Big Brutus." At 160 feet tall and 11 million pounds, it is the second-largest electric mining shovel in the world. To reach layers of coal inside the earth, huge pits were dug, and Big Brutus did the digging. It could fill three railroad cars with one giant scoop. By the 1970s it became too expensive to run and too big to get rid of. Rather than allow its bulk to rust away, the people of West Mineral painted it orange and turned it into a museum.

Big Brutus is retired and now serves as a mining museum.

PLACES TO SEE

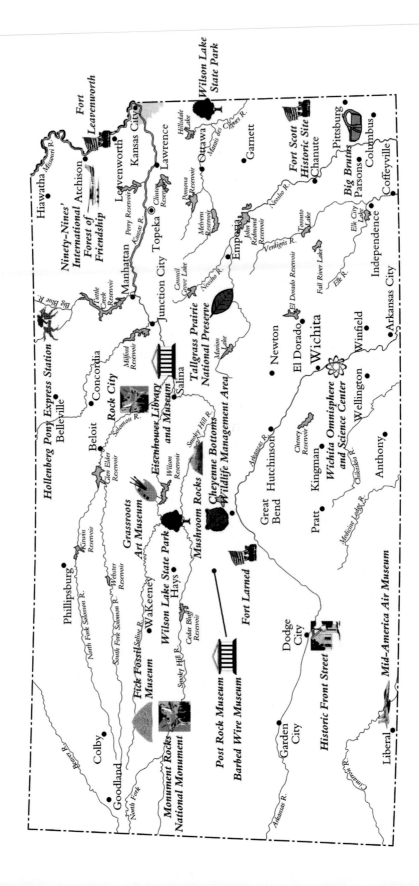

Hollenberg Pony Express Station

Hiawatha

Ninety-Nines' International Forest of Friendship

Fort Leavenworth

Wilson Lake State Park

Belleville

Atchison

Leavenworth

Kansas City

Manhattan

Lawrence

Topeka

Hillsdale Lake

Garnett

Ottawa

Rock City

Concordia

Junction City

Beloit

Salina

Tallgrass Prairie National Preserve

Emporia

Fort Scott Historic Site

Pittsburg

Chanute

Big Brutus

Columbus

Parsons

Coffeyville

Phillipsburg

Grassroots Art Museum

Eisenhower Library and Museum

Cheyenne Bottoms Wildlife Management Area

Newton

El Dorado

Wichita

Independence

Arkansas City

Colby

Goodland

Fick Fossil Museum

Mushroom Rocks

Wilson Lake State Park

Hays

WaKeeney

Great Bend

Hutchinson

Wichita Omnisphere and Science Center

Winfield

Wellington

Anthony

Monument Rocks National Monument

Post Rock Museum

Barbed Wire Museum

Fort Larned

Dodge City

Pratt

Kingman

Garden City

Historic Front Street

Mid-America Air Museum

Liberal

Missouri R.

Kansas R.

Perry Reservoir

Clinton Reservoir

Pomona Reservoir

Melvern Reservoir

Marais des Cygnes R.

Neosho R.

John Redmond Reservoir

Verdigris R.

Toronto Lake

Fall River Lake

Elk City Lake

Elk R.

Tuttle Creek Reservoir

Big Blue R.

Milford Reservoir

Council Grove Lake

Neosho R.

Marion Lake

El Dorado Reservoir

Arkansas R.

Cheney Reservoir

Chikaskia R.

Medicine Lodge R.

Glen Elder Reservoir

Wilson Reservoir

Solomon R.

Smoky Hill R.

Kirwin Reservoir

North Fork Solomon R.

Webster Reservoir

South Fork Solomon R.

Saline R.

Cedar Bluff Reservoir

Smoky Hill R.

Beaver R.

North Fork

Arkansas R.

Cimarron R.

They let the pits surrounding it fill with water and stocked them with fish. Now Big Brutus towers over visiting families while they fish, swim, and picnic.

Farther north and west, in La Crosse, you will find the Post Rock Museum and the Barbed Wire Museum. When the pioneers first settled on the plains, they lived in fear of being trampled by marauding cattle. Without wood, they had no way to build fences. So when barbed wire was invented in the 1870s, the pioneers welcomed the chance to protect themselves. They carved fence posts from limestone, which they called post rock. Then they strung the prickly wire between the posts, success-fully thwarting stampedes. In the Barbed Wire Museum you will see more than five hundred types of the "devil's rope." There are single strands and parallel strands, double knots and triple twists, as well as splicers and other tools used to twist and string it.

For a truly different experience, drive past beautiful Wilson Lake State Park to the whimsical town of Lucas. There the Grassroots Art Center exhibits folk art made by midwestern artists. It features the art of Inez Mar-shall who, though disabled, sculpted 400-pound pieces of limestone into works such as a Model-T Ford with working headlights and a nearly life-sized covered wagon and mule team. Or walk a few blocks to Florence Deeble's house. A schoolteacher born in 1906, Deeble spent more than seventy years turning her backyard into a sculpture garden filled with concrete, crystals, and statues collected during her world travels. Walk a little farther and you will inevitably stop in front of Samuel Dinsmoor's Garden of Eden. In 1907 the Civil War veteran began work on a cement sculpture garden. It features some 150 concrete statues, including the Statue of Liberty, an American flag and, of course, Adam and Eve. It's quite a sight, welcoming about ten thousand visitors a year.

LET'S HOPE IT NEVER ROLLS AWAY!

Cawker City in north-central Kansas is home to what is reportedly the largest ball of twine in the world. With a 40-foot circumference, the massive orb contains nearly 8 million feet of twine! Farmer Frank Stoeber started it in 1953 as a fun way to dispose of the twine used to bind bales of hay. Before long the ball got too big to fit through the barn door, so Stoeber donated it to the city, and it was put on display. Each August the city holds a twine-a-thon, where people come to wrap more string around the ever-growing orb. You do not have to wait for the festival to get in on the fun. Visitors to Cawker may get a bit of string to add to the 9-ton ball.

Concrete statues are the main attraction at the Garden of Eden.

Samuel Dinsmoor's Garden of Eden is also a perfect example of what makes Kansas special and why those who call Kansas home couldn't imagine living anywhere else. "Kansas is a great place to visit," says thirteen-year-old Tony Ochs, "especially if you love barbecue, basketball, tornadoes, wheat, and sunflowers." Seventh-grader DaVaughn Pelts puts it, simply, "Kansas is my favorite place to be."

THE FLAG: The Kansas flag consists of the state seal against a blue background. Below the seal is the word Kansas. *Above it is a sunflower, the state flower. The flag was adopted in 1927.*

THE SEAL: The state seal, adopted in 1861, shows a landscape that includes a wagon train and two Indians hunting buffalo. In the foreground is a man plowing a field, which represents the importance of agriculture to the state. In the background is a steamboat on a river, symbolizing commerce. Above the scene are thirty-four stars, signifying Kansas's place as the thirty-fourth state.

State Survey

Statehood: January 29, 1861

Origin of Name: From the Kansa Indians, whose name means "people of the south wind"

Nickname: Sunflower State

Capital: Topeka

Motto: To the Stars through Difficulties

Bird: Western meadowlark

Flower: Sunflower

Tree: Cottonwood

Insect: Honeybee

Animal: Buffalo

Reptile: Ornate box turtle

Amphibian: Barred tiger salamander

Sunflower

Buffalo

HOME ON THE RANGE

In 1873 a prairie doctor named Higley Brewster of Smith County, Kansas, had a medical office in his typical sod house on the prairie. One day Brewster looked about and was moved by the beauty of the land. He was so overwhelmed that he wrote a poem, which when set to music by Daniel E. Kelly, became this most famous of all western songs. It was adopted as the official state song in 1947.

Words by Higley Brewster   **Music by Daniel E. Kelly**

GEOGRAPHY

Highest Point: 4,039 feet above sea level, at Mount Sunflower

Lowest Point: 679 feet, along the Verdigris River in Montgomery County

Area: 82,282 square miles

Greatest Distance North to South: 206 miles

Greatest Distance East to West: 408 miles

Bordering States: Nebraska to the north, Missouri to the east, Oklahoma to the south, and Colorado to the west

Hottest Recorded Temperature: 121 ºF in Fredonia on July 18, 1936, and in Alton on July 24, 1936

Coldest Recorded Temperature: –40 ºF in Lebanon on February 13, 1905

Average Annual Precipitation: 27 inches

Major Rivers: Arkansas, Big Blue, Cimarron, Kansas, Marais des Cygnes, Missouri, Neosho, Republican, Saline, Smoky Hill, Solomon, Verdigris

Major Lakes: Cedar Bluff, Cheney, Fall River, John Redmond, Kanopolis, Kirwin, McKinney, Milford, Pomona, Toronto, Tuttle Creek, Webster

Trees: ash, black walnut, cottonwood, elm, hickory, locust, maple, oak, pecan, sycamore, willow

Wild Plants: aster, blue grama, bluestem, columbine, goldenrod, morning glory, sunflower, tumbleweed, verbena

Animals: beaver, coyote, muskrat, opossum, prairie dog, pronghorn, rabbit, raccoon, rattlesnake

Birds: blue jay, cardinal, crow, duck, hawk, meadowlark, pheasant, prairie chicken, quail, robin, sparrow, wild turkey, woodpecker

Fish: bass, bluegill, carp, catfish, crappie, walleye

Endangered Animals and Fish: American peregrine falcon, bald eagle, black-capped vireo, black-footed ferret, Eskimo curlew, gray bat, least tern, pallid sturgeon, piping plover, Topeka shiner, whooping crane

TIMELINE

Kansas History

1500s The Kansa, Osage, Pawnee, Wichita, and Plains Apache Indians live in present-day Kansas.

1541 Spaniard Francisco Vásquez de Coronado leads an expedition into Kansas in search of a legendary city of gold.

1673 French explorers arrive in present-day Kansas.

Black-footed ferret

1803 Kansas becomes part of U.S. territory through the Louisiana Purchase.

1821 The Santa Fe Trail is established, from Franklin, Missouri, to Santa Fe, New Mexico, crossing through Kansas.

1827 Fort Leavenworth, the first U.S. outpost in present-day Kansas, is established.

1830 Congress passes the Indian Removal Bill, forcing twenty-seven tribes from the East into Kansas.

1850s Violence erupts frequently over the issue of slavery, earning the territory the nickname Bleeding Kansas.

1854 Land taken back from the Indians is opened to white settlement; Kansas Territory is created.

1855 The territorial legislature provides free schools for white children.

1859 Kansas's first library opens in Vinland.

1861 Kansas becomes the thirty-fourth state; the Civil War begins.

1863 Most of Lawrence is burned by Confederate raider William C. Quantrill.

Late 1860s Kansas towns such as Dodge City and Abilene become booming cow towns, shipping Texas longhorn cattle to other parts of the country.

1870s Mennonite emigrants from Russia begin planting Turkey Red winter wheat, which soon becomes the dominant variety grown in the state.

1887 Susanna Madora Salter is elected mayor of Argonia, becoming the first female mayor in the United States.

1892 Oil is discovered near Neodesha.

1903 Kansas state capitol in Topeka is completed at a cost of $3.2 billion.

1905 Helium is discovered near Dexter.

1934–1935 Drought and dust storms sweep through the Great Plains; many Kansas farmers falling victim to the Dust Bowl.

1937 Kansan Amelia Earhart's plane goes down over the Pacific Ocean on the final leg of a historic round-the-world flight.

1941 The United States enters World War II.

1952 Kansan Dwight D. Eisenhower is elected president.

1954 The U.S. Supreme Court declares segregation in public schools illegal in *Brown vs. Board of Education of Topeka*.

1955 Powerful F5 tornado strikes Udall, killing eighty-three people and destroying the town.

1967 The Kansas City Chiefs professional football team plays in the first Super Bowl, losing to the Green Bay Packers 35–10.

1985 The Kansas City Royals professional baseball team wins its first World Series title, beating the St. Louis Cardinals four games to three.

1986 Kansas voters approve the creation of a state lottery.

1990 Joan Finney is elected the first female governor of Kansas.

1993 The Great Flood damages or destroys nearly one-fifth of the state's total farmland; crop and property losses top $450 million.

1995 Casino gambling on American-Indian reservations is legalized.

1996 Kansas senator Bob Dole runs for U.S. president and is defeated by Bill Clinton.

2005 Kansas's largest wind farm, Elk River, opens in the Flint Hills, making Kansas one of the top-ten states in the production of renewable energy.

2007 An F5 tornado tears through Greensburg, demolishing most of the town and killing nine people; massive floods hit southeast Kansas.

ECONOMY

Agricultural Products: beef cattle, corn, hay, hogs, milk, sorghum, soybeans, sugar beets, wheat

Wheat

Manufactured Products: airplanes, chemicals, farm equipment, food products, printed materials, railroad cars, rubber products

Natural Resources: coal, helium, limestone, natural gas, oil, salt

Business and Trade: banking, insurance, transportation, wholesale and retail trade

CALENDAR OF CELEBRATIONS

International Pancake Race Each February women in Liberal and women in Olney, England, compete in this 415-yard footrace while carrying a pancake on a skillet.

Wichita River Festival The people of Wichita take advantage of their beautiful May days with this festival that includes hot air balloons, evening concerts, and fireworks displays.

Wah-Shun-Gah Days Dancing, crafts, a Santa Fe Trail ride, and even an antique tractor pull are all part of the festivities at the Kaw powwow held in Council Grove in June.

Twin Rivers Festival Emporia celebrates the arts in June with dances, concerts, arts-and-crafts displays, and lots of children's activities.

Beef Empire Days Beef is big business in Kansas. In June Garden City holds an educational festival that features fun events such as rodeos, a pancake feast, and a cowboy poetry reading. There's also the Beef Expo in Hutchinson, and each August, Emporia hosts the Flint Hills Beef Fest.

Fiesta Mexicana Each July Topeka's Mexican-American population puts on one of the largest Hispanic festivals in the Midwest. There is a parade, folk dancing, games, traditional foods, and even a jalapeño-pepper-eating contest for the brave.

Pretty Prairie Rodeo The state's largest rodeo is held in Pretty Prairie each July. The rodeo draws big crowds, and the top two hundred cowboys on the circuit vie for $50,000 in prize money.

Lenexa Spinach Fest Lenexa was once the largest spinach producer in the world. Each September the town holds a festival honoring spinach, which includes the world's largest spinach salad (using 500 pounds of spinach), spinach milkshakes, spinach tortillas, and hats made out of vegetables.

Pioneer Days Hays remembers its pioneer past every September with demonstrations of skills such as rope making, whittling, and post-stone cutting.

Renaissance Festival Every weekend in September and October Bonner Springs holds a Renaissance Festival. Visitors munch on turkey drumsticks while jesters cavort and knights on horseback try to topple each other while jousting.

Renaissance Festival

Fall Festival North Newton honors its Mennonite past in October with a celebration that includes crafts, athletic competitions, and cooking demonstrations. Don't miss the verenike (cheese-filled pastries) or the New Year's cookies.

Lucia Fest Lindsborg welcomes the Christmas season with this traditional Swedish festival that features music, folk dancing, and lots of delicious Swedish baked goods. Its highlight is the crowning of St. Lucia, who wears a crown of candles.

STATE STARS

Annette Bening (1958–   ) is an actor known for her Oscar-nominated performances in *Being Julia* (2004), *American Beauty* (1999), and *The Grifters* (1990). Bening began her career on the New York stage, earning a Tony nomination for her role in *Coastal Disturbances* before turning her attention to film. Bening has appeared in a wide variety of movies, from *Mars Attacks!* to *The American President*. She was born in Topeka.

Annette Bening

Gwendolyn Brooks (1917–2000) was a poet who was the first African American to win a Pulitzer Prize. Born in Topeka, Brooks published her first book of poems, *A Street in Bronzeville,* in 1945. She quickly gained acclaim for her intense and often witty depictions of black urban life. Brooks earned the 1950 Pulitzer Prize for *Annie Allen.*

William Burroughs (1914–1997) was a writer famous for his experimental novels, which often include grotesque imagery and dark humor. His best-known work, *Naked Lunch,* brilliantly depicts the paranoid and almost mad mind-set of drug addicts. Born in Missouri, Burroughs lived much of his later life in Lawrence, Kansas.

Clyde Cessna (1879–1954), an airplane manufacturer, was born in Iowa and grew up in Kansas. For a while Cessna worked as an auto mechanic, but after seeing his first air show, in 1910, he was hooked on planes, and he built his first plane that winter. In 1917 he became the first airplane manufacturer in Wichita, which had become a hub of aviation activity. Cessna eventually built the first plane in the country that had no struts or wires connecting the wings to the body. In 1927 he founded the Cessna Aircraft Company.

Walter Chrysler (1875–1940), an automaker, was born in Wamego and grew up in Ellis. Chrysler began his career as a railroad mechanic. He later worked for Buick and General Motors before founding the Chrysler Corporation in 1925. It eventually became one of the world's largest automobile companies.

Gwendolyn Brooks

Buffalo Bill Cody (1846–1917) was a legend of the Wild West. He was born in Iowa, but his family soon became among the first pioneers to settle Kansas. Cody's adventures began early. At age fourteen he became a Pony Express rider, and during the Civil War he was a scout for the Union army. After the war the Kansas Pacific Railroad hired him to provide buffalo meat for the crews laying track. Killing as many as two thousand buffalo a month, Cody earned his nickname. In later years Cody became famous as a showman, organizing the incredibly popular Wild West Show, which presented a romanticized view of life in the West.

Amelia Earhart (1897–1937), a native of Atchison, was a pioneering pilot. She was the first woman to fly across the Atlantic, the first woman to fly solo across the Atlantic, and the first person to fly solo across the Pacific. Her plane disappeared in 1937 while she was attempting to fly around the world.

Amelia Earhart

Dwight D. Eisenhower (1890–1969) was the thirty-fourth president of the United States. Eisenhower was born in Texas and moved to Abilene, Kansas, as a baby. He attended West Point Military Academy and worked his way up through the army ranks to become a general. During World War II Eisenhower commanded all Allied troops in Europe and accepted the German surrender. During his two terms as president he ended the Korean War and began work on the interstate highway system, the largest construction project in history.

Dwight Eisenhower

Wild Bill Hickok (1837–1876) was a famous lawman of the Wild West. Hickok was born in Illinois and moved to Kansas at about age eighteen. He worked as a stagecoach driver on the Santa Fe Trail and served as a Union spy and scout during the Civil War. His first law enforcement job was in Monticello, Kansas. He later became a U.S. marshall in Fort Riley, Hays, and Abilene, gaining fame for bringing peace to these lawless towns. Hickok was eventually shot and killed in a saloon in Deadwood, South Dakota.

Dennis Hopper (1936–   ) is an actor known for playing rebellious, oftentimes crazed characters. He became widely known in 1969, when he wrote, directed, and starred in *Easy Rider*. This film, about a cross-country motorcycle trip, became a big hit and an emblem of the 1960s counterculture. Hopper was born in Dodge City.

Langston Hughes (1902–1967) was an influential African-American writer who gained prominence as part of the Harlem Renaissance, a flowering of the arts that took place during the 1920s in New York's most famous black community. Hughes is best remembered for his poems, such as "The Negro Speaks of Rivers" and "Harlem," which incorporate everyday language and the rhythms of black music. Hughes spent much of his childhood in Lawrence and Topeka.

William Inge (1913–1973), a renowned playwright, was born in Independence and attended the University of Kansas. In plays such as *Bus Stop*, *Picnic*, and *Come Back, Little Sheba*, Inge explored the

Langston Hughes

hopes and frustrations of people living in small towns. All of these plays were turned into films. Inge also wrote directly for the screen, most famously *Splendor in the Grass*, which earned him an Academy Award for Best Original Screenplay.

Walter Johnson (1887–1946) is considered by many to be baseball's greatest pitcher ever. Johnson, who was nicknamed Big Train because he threw so fast, was born in Humboldt. In his twenty years with the Washington Senators, he won 416 games, the second-highest total in baseball history. He threw 110 shutouts, a major league record, and led the American League in strikeouts 12 times. Johnson was elected to the Baseball Hall of Fame in 1936.

Nancy Kassebaum (1932–   ) was the first female U.S. senator from Kansas. The daughter of Alfred Landon, the governor of Kansas and a 1936 Republican presidential candidate, she was born in Topeka. In 1978 Kassebaum was elected to the U.S. Senate, becoming the first female senator elected to a full term who did not succeed her husband in either house of Congress.

Buster Keaton (1895–1966) was a silent-film director and actor famous for his deadpan expressions, extraordinary timing, and comic sense. In such masterpieces as *Sherlock, Jr.*; *The Navigator*; and *The General*, Keaton played characters who could endure any frustration and were oblivious to danger. After the silent film era ended, Keaton's career declined, and he was forced to play minor roles. He was born in Piqua.

Walter Johnson

Martina McBride (1966–) is one of America's top country music singers. Beginning in the 1990s McBride racked up 22 top-ten singles, including *Wild Angels* and *A Broken Wing*, and has since sold more than 16 million records. McBride is known for lending her powerful voice to songs that speak out about social issues, such as domestic abuse. The four-time Country Music Association Female Vocalist of the Year was born in Sharon.

Hattie McDaniel (1895–1952), from Wichita, was the first African American to win an Academy Award. Her 1939 performance as Mammy in *Gone with the Wind* earned her a Best Supporting Actress Oscar. This daughter of a former slave was also the first African American to attend the Academy Award ceremonies as a guest, not a servant.

Carry Nation (1846–1911) was a leader in the movement to outlaw alcohol. Nation, who was born in Kentucky, was the widow of an alcoholic. She eventually settled in Medicine Lodge, Kansas, where she began giving lectures on the evils of liquor. She gradually became more radical and began destroying saloons with a hatchet. Though she was arrested thirty times, she inspired others to fight for Prohibition.

Sara Paretsky (1947–) is a mystery writer who created the strong, independent, and witty female private eye V. I. Warshawski. Paretsky's novels, such as *Burn Marks* and *Blood Shot*, are notable for being murder mysteries that also deal with social problems. Paretsky grew up in Lawrence.

Martina McBride

Charlie Parker (1920–1955), a Kansas City native, was the greatest and most influential saxophone player of all time. Parker helped found the bebop style of jazz, which was fast, complex, and rhythmically inventive. To this day, saxophonists learning to play copy his improvisations. Parker, who was nicknamed Bird, is responsible for such classic songs as "Ornithology" and "Bird's Nest."

Gordon Parks (1912–2006) was a groundbreaking African-American photographer, filmmaker, artist, writer, and composer. After gaining recognition for his photographs of poor people during the 1940s, Parks became prominent as a photographer for *Life* magazine. In 1969 he directed *The Learning Tree*, becoming the first African American to direct a Hollywood motion picture. Parks was born in Fort Scott, the youngest of fifteen children.

Gale Sayers (1943–   ) is one of the greatest running backs in football history. Sayers was born in Wichita and attended the University of Kansas, where his speed and dazzling moves earned him the nickname the Kansas Comet. During his rookie season with the Chicago Bears, he set a league record of twenty-two touchdowns and once scored a record six touchdowns in one game. Although his career was cut short by injury, he twice led the league in rushing. In 1977, at age thirty-four, he became the youngest player ever inducted into the Pro Football Hall of Fame.

Rex Stout (1886–1975) was a writer who created Nero Wolfe, one of the mystery genre's greatest detectives. Wolfe loves gourmet food and orchids and seldom leaves his house. Instead he sends his amiable, wise-guy assistant, Archie Goodwin, to do the legwork. Stout, who wrote more than forty Nero Wolfe books, grew up in Wakarusa.

Gale Sayers

Clyde Tombaugh (1906–1997), an astronomer, was born in Illinois and later moved with his family to a farm in western Kansas. It was there, in 1925, that he built his first telescope. After studying the planets through another telescope he had made himself, Tombaugh took a job at Lowell Observatory in Arizona looking for a ninth planet in the solar system. In 1930 he discovered what he thought was a new planet—Pluto.

Lynette Woodard (1959–   ), a native of Wichita, is one of the best female basketball players of all time. At the University of Kansas she broke twenty-four of the thirty-two records kept for women's college basketball, including scoring a record average of 26.3 points per game during each of her four years of college. Woodard later joined the comic but extremely talented Harlem Globetrotters, becoming the first woman ever to play professional basketball with men.

TOUR THE STATE

Historic Front Street (Dodge City) For a taste of the Old West visit this reconstruction of two Dodge City blocks from the 1870s.

Mid America Air Museum (Liberal) Get an up-close view of nearly seventy flying machines at this museum, including a 1929 Pietenpol, which is powered by a Model-A automobile engine.

Fick Fossil and History Museum (Oakley) In addition to thousands of sharks' teeth and other fossils, this museum displays cattle brands, a sod house, and railroad equipment.

Dodge City

Cathedral of the Plains (Victoria) This beautiful limestone church was built by German-Russian settlers in the early twentieth century.

Wilson State Park (Russell) A region of rugged rock arches, steep barren hills, and deep canyons, this is the perfect place for hiking, fishing, boating, and picnicking.

Cheyenne Bottoms Wildlife Management Area (Great Bend) Wildlife lovers come from all over to visit the largest inland marsh in the United States, where nearly 15 million shorebirds spend the winter.

Rock City (Minneapolis) Large sandstone rocks rise from the prairie at this site. Some are almost perfectly round, others look like pyramids, and still others are balanced precariously atop one another.

Wichita Omnisphere and Science Center (Wichita) The highlight of this science museum is the planetarium's fascinating star show. Enjoy hands-on exhibits covering such subjects as optical illusions and electricity.

Hollenberg Pony Express Station (Hanover) Built in 1857, this is the only unaltered Pony Express station that still stands on its original site.

Missouri River Queen (Kansas City) For a relaxing afternoon, take a cruise on the Missouri River in this turn-of-the-century paddle-wheel boat.

Cathedral of the Plains

Old Depot Museum (Ottawa) Housed in an old railroad depot, this historical museum features a 1918 locomotive and exhibits on the eras of Bleeding Kansas and the Civil War.

Big Brutus (West Mineral) This fifteen-story-high orange mining shovel is now the centerpiece of a park filled with lovely lakes and picnic areas.

Fort Scott National Historic Site (Fort Scott) On a visit to this fort, built in the 1840s, you can tour a hospital, officers' quarters, and a bakery.

Kansas Cosmosphere and Space Center (Hutchinson) This air and space museum features the actual *Apollo 13* command module, a replica of the space shuttle *Endeavor*, and the largest collection of space suits in the world.

Mine Creek Battlefield (Pleasanton) On this prairie in east-central Kansas, one of the largest cavalry battles of the Civil War took place in 1864. Walk the trails and go through the museum to discover how a Union force defeated a Confederate cavalry three times its size.

Amelia Earhart Birthplace Museum (Atchison) Tour the house where this great American pioneer of aviation was born and spent much of her happy childhood. (The house belonged to her grandparents.)

Brown vs. Board of Education National Historic Site (Topeka) Learn about the civil rights movement of the 1960s and what it took to end legal segregation in American public schools.

Kansas Cosmosphere and Space Center

Nicodemus National Historic Site (Nicodemus) Explore this pioneer town, settled in 1877 by former slaves, whose descendants continue to live and work there today.

Dwight D. Eisenhower Center (Abilene) Tour the presidential museum and library, and the Eisenhower home, located in the hometown of the thirty-fourth president of the United States.

Kansas Museum of History (Topeka) Experience the rich history of Kansas firsthand. See a full-scale Cheyenne tepee, a covered wagon, and an 1880 locomotive made for the Atchison, Topeka, and Santa Fe Railroad.

Augusta Air Museum (Augusta) This museum features more than ten thousand military and aviation artifacts, including letters, uniforms, and more than two hundred model airplanes. Check out the Penguin training airplane that dates back to the 1920s and the German submarine helicopter.

State Capitol (Topeka) Take a guided tour to view the Senate and House chambers, learn more about John Steuart Curry's extraordinary murals, and decide whether or not the legends about ghosts haunting the building are true.

FUN FACTS

Kansas is named for the Kansa, or Kaw, a group of American Indians that once roamed the region's vast plains and prairies. The word means "people of the South wind" (only Massachusetts, Montana, and Wyoming clock stronger winds than Kansas).

Dwight D. Eisenhower Center

Kansas is second only to Texas in the number of meteorites found there. In October 2005 a giant meteorite was dug up in rural Kiowa County in south-central Kansas, weighing a world-record 1,400 pounds.

Take a dip in one of the largest swimming pools in the world. Garden City's municipal pool is as long as a football field and holds 2.8 million gallons of water.

The first national hamburger chain got its start when Walter Anderson opened the White Castle restaurant in Wichita in 1921.

In 1866 U.S. Army Lieutenant Colonel George Custer led the famous 7th Cavalry Regiment at Fort Riley in northeastern Kansas. Ten years later Custer and all 260 men under his command were killed in a clash with the Sioux and Cheyenne in Montana. The only cavalry survivor of the Battle of the Little Big Horn was a horse named Comanche.

Coffeyville restaurant owner Omar Knedlik invented the first slushy drinks and the ICEE machine. Brainfreeze!

Find Out More

There's so much to learn about Kansas. Ask for these titles at your library or bookstore. Be sure to visit the Web sites that follow, too.

BOOKS

Ames, John Edwards. *The Real Deadwood: True Life Histories of Wild Bill Hickok, Calamity Jane, Outlaw Towns, and Other Characters of the Lawless West*. New York: Chamberlain Bros., 2004.

Birkner, Michael J. *Dwight D. Eisenhower: America's 34th President*. Danbury, CT: Children's Press, 2005.

Burke John. *Amelia Earhart: Flying Solo*. New York: Sterling, 2007.

Delano, Patricia. *Kansas: Off the Beaten Path*. Guilford, CT: The Globe Pequot Press, 2005.

Olson, Nathan. *Tornadoes*. Mankato, MN: Capstone Press, 2006.

Steele, Christy. *Pioneer Life in the American West*. Milwaukee: World Almanac Library, 2005.

Stewart, Mark. *The Kansas City Royals*. Chicago: Norwood House Press, 2008.

Young, Jeff C. *Bleeding Kansas and the Violent Clash Over Slavery in the Heartland*. Berkeley Heights, NJ: MyReportLinks.com Books, 2006.

WEB SITES

Kansas State Library, Blue Skyways

http://skyways.lib.ks.us/kansas

Blue Skyways is a shared information service among Kansas's state libraries. This site offers links to state museums, government organizations, schools, and the home pages of hundreds of towns and cities across Kansas.

Kansas State Historical Society

http://www.kshs.org

Log on to learn more about the famous (and infamous) people who made Kansas what it is. View a historical timeline, learn fun facts, see maps, and plan your visit to the Sunflower State.

Kansas State Government

http://www.kansas.gov

Everything you ever wanted to know about Kansas state and local governments can be found here. You can see what the Kansas legislature is doing right now and link to the governor's Web site.

National Park Service

http://home.nps.gov/state/ks

Explore the rivers, parks, national trails, and monuments that make Kansas such a fascinating place to visit.

The Nature Conservancy

http://www.nature.org/wherewework/northamerica/states/kansas

The Nature Conservancy works to preserve valuable ecosystems around the world. At this Web site learn what is being done to protect Kansas's tallgrass prairies, mixed prairies, and other vanishing landscapes.

Index

Page numbers in **boldface** are illustrations and charts.

ABOUT THE AUTHORS

Ruth Bjorklund is a youth services librarian living on an island near Seattle, Washington, with her husband, two children, three cats, and two dogs. Some of her best friends, both old and new, live in the great state of Kansas.

A former television weather forecaster, Trudi Strain Trueit has always been awed by the wild weather of Kansas and "tornado alley." She has written more than forty nonfiction children's titles on various subjects from reptiles to journaling to video games. She is also the author of the popular *Julep O'Toole* (Dutton) fiction series for middle-grade readers. Trueit holds a Bachelor of Arts degree in broadcast journalism from Pacific Lutheran University in Tacoma, Washington. Born and raised in Seattle, she still lives in the Pacific Northwest with her husband, Bill. To learn more about Trueit and her books, visit www.truditrueit.com.